Jr. High Retreats & Lock-Ins

By Karen Dockrey

Loveland, Colorado

Jr. High Retreats & Lock-Ins

Copyright © 1990 by Karen Dockrey

First Printing

Credits
Edited by Michael D. Warden
Designed by Judy Atwood Bienick and Jill Bendykowski
Illustrations by Dennis Jones

Library of Congress Cataloging-in-Publication Data
Dockrey, Karen, 1955-
   Jr. high retreats & lock-ins / by Karen Dockrey.
     p. cm.
   Includes bibliographical references.
   1. Retreats for youth. 2. Teenagers—Religious life.
  3. Teenagers—Conduct of life. I. Title. II. Title: Junior high retreats and lock-ins.
   BV4531.2.D617 1990
   269'.63—dc20
                                  90-31969
                                      CIP

ISBN 0-931529-73-5
Printed in the United States of America

Contents

SECTION 1: Leading Successful Retreats and Lock-Ins With Junior Highers

Chapter 1: Why Retreats and Lock-Ins Work 7
Chapter 2: Planning a Retreat or Lock-In 16
Chapter 3: Training Workers for Retreats and Lock-Ins 32

SECTION 2: Junior High Retreats

Retreat 1: Liking Myself So I Can Like You
Self-esteem. 43
Retreat 2: Friendship Gardens
Building friendships 57
Retreat 3: "Why Can't My Parents Understand Me?"
Improving family relationships 73
Retreat 4: God's Good Gift of Sex
Making smart choices about sex 86
Retreat 5: Responding to Feelings
Handling emotions...101
Retreat 6: Back-to-School Retreat
Enjoying school...115

SECTION 3: Junior High Lock-Ins

Lock-In 1: Building My Own Faith
Developing your own faith...129
Lock-In 2: Discovering and Using My Spiritual Gifts
Spiritual gifts 141
Lock-In 3: Loneliness and Looks
Finding acceptance 155
Lock-In 4: Peer Pressure
Harnessing the power of peer pressure 166
Lock-In 5: My Place to Belong
Group unity 176
Lock-In 6: Life After Death
Eternal life 187

Dedication

Dedicated to Jeanne,
who reminds me to be still and enjoy God's presence.

SECTION 1:

Leading Successful Retreats and Lock-Ins With Junior Highers

CHAPTER 1

Why Retreats and Lock-Ins Work

There's something about getting away that brings out the best in kids. They tend to drop their defenses, share true feelings, get honest with God and grow closer to each other. You can do the same studies at church but not with the same impact. Retreats take work, planning and energy. But they're worth it because time away from home encourages spiritual, personal and group growth in ways few other events can.

With solid advance planning, lock-ins can also be effective spiritual growth experiences. Three a.m. fights provide great opportunities to teach conflict resolution. Being locked up with a group of rowdy junior highers can bring out the best as well as the worst. The extended time together can create an atmosphere for group-building and spiritual growth.

But exactly what is a retreat or a lock-in? And how are they different? Let's look at each event to answer these questions.

WHAT'S A RETREAT?

A retreat is a gathering of people for study and fellowship in a setting away from home. It's a *retreat* from routine schedules and surroundings to regroup and re-energize. Most retreats take place in secluded settings where kids can be close to nature. They may last two or three days—even four on occasion. A retreat's primary goal is to remove normal daily distractions to allow kids to focus on spiritual growth.

For junior highers, retreats generally focus on a subject or are used as a planning time. Either way, retreats often draw kids closer to God and to each other. Most junior highers who go on retreats return more unified with a greater sense of belonging. Junior high retreats usually focus on helping kids in these three areas:

- growth in their relationship with God;
- growth in understanding of a topic; and
- growth in unity.

WHAT'S A LOCK-IN?

Lock-ins are all-night events where kids come together for fun and intense learning. Lock-ins hold similar goals as a retreat, but usually take place at a church or other site. Because kids aren't as secluded, they don't always experience as much spiritual or group growth as they might at a retreat. But lock-ins offer the advantages of a local site, less planning, and less time for the event itself. They can be held more often and with less money.

Lock-ins often last 12 hours—such as from 8 p.m. to 8 a.m.—with no kids coming or leaving between. They're locked in for the duration. Sometimes groups bend this rule, allowing late arrivals and early departures. This may allow more junior highers to come, but it also interrupts the continuity of the experience—both for kids who come and go, and those who're there for the duration.

Because each activity in a lock-in experience builds on the one before it, I recommend the "locked-in philosophy," requiring full-time or no-time attendance. Kids respect events with consistent requirements and may value the lock-in more because of this rule.

Many lock-ins are stay-up-all-night events. I, however, schedule at least a few hours of sleep to keep kids from getting on each

---

Retreat or Lock-in?

Should you schedule a retreat or a lock-in for your kids? Consider these general characteristics to help your decision.

Retreat	**Lock-In**
● It occurs in a secluded setting.	● It occurs in a home church setting.
● Kids tend to expect deeper study.	● Kids tend to expect fun and games.
● Kids have more time for study and worship.	● Kids have less time for study but the study is more focused.
● It's usually more expensive.	● It's usually less expensive.
● Kids expect to sleep most of the night.	● Kids expect to stay up all or most of the night.
● It requires extensive planning.	● It can be done more spontaneously.

other's nerves and to preserve leaders' sanity. Most junior highers will agree to sleep at 3 a.m.—as long as everyone else has to do it too.

BENEFITS FROM AN ADULT PERSPECTIVE

Retreats and lock-ins meet real needs of real kids. Leaders say junior highers' greatest needs are:
- more self-confidence;
- more meaningful faith;
- better family relationships;
- better understanding of who they are;
- straight answers to honest questions;
- help in coping with problems; and
- fun.[1]

Retreats and lock-ins can meet these needs in the following ways.

They provide opportunities for kids to succeed. Success builds self-confidence and helps kids discover who they are—or more accurately, who they're becoming.

They allow kids to relate to God in a loving atmosphere. Retreat settings often enable kids to *feel* God's presence rather than just talk about it. Develop an atmosphere that encourages kids to experience God's presence.

They provide opportunities for late-night talks. Big questions tend to materialize at night. When the lights go out, junior highers may ask questions or reveal fears they'd never share with the lights on. This is the main reason for cabin devotions. With a counselor's help, junior highers can discover God's answers to important life questions.

They emphasize problem-centered study. The best retreats for junior high kids focus on felt needs—felt by junior highers, not imposed by adults. These needs frequently center around family, friends, God, love and dating.

They include group-building games. Junior highers love to be together and want to feel a part of a group. The best games build on this need and encourage unity. They balance competition with cooperation. They help each junior higher feel important and competent.

BENEFITS FROM A TEENAGER'S PERSPECTIVE

Retreats and lock-ins attract kids for several reasons. Behind all the attractions is the belief the event will meet a need in their lives.

Kids themselves say their greatest needs are:
● responding to peer pressure;
● making good grades;
● gaining popularity and acceptance;
● getting along with parents;
● growing up;
● making money;
● coping with stress;
● choosing friends;
● dating;
● overcoming boredom or depression; and
● setting goals.[2]

Retreats and lock-ins can meet junior highers' needs by:
● addressing kids' felt needs in an atmosphere of honesty and acceptance;
● providing positive peer pressure;
● helping kids discover that their peers have similar problems with families, friends, the opposite sex and other relationships;
● encouraging kids to work together to discover solutions to mutual problems;
● filling "boredom weekends" with fun activities;
● offering rich opportunities for togetherness and group-building; and
● helping kids set goals together for church activities or personal growth.

KEYS TO SUCCESS

I started as youth minister in a church with about 20 kids and anxiously anticipated my first retreat. I chose a subject, booked a site, composed a menu and publicized the retreat. Parents donated the food we needed. I covered every detail.

On the day of the retreat only four kids showed. We waited a little longer and still no one came. Four kids and four counselors. What went wrong?

Although I'd covered most of the important facets that go into planning a retreat, I'd overlooked one of the most crucial keys to success. What was it?

Key #1: Involvement—Reread that first paragraph. *I* did all the

Why Not Combine?

Why not just combine your junior high retreat or lock-in with your senior high one? If you're doing it purely for convenience, don't. But there are good reasons to combine junior high and senior high kids—especially if you want to build group unity, save money or have more kids attend. The down side of combining groups is it's harder to meet kids' different spiritual, social, physical and emotional needs. Consider these additional pros and cons for combining groups, and make a decision guided by God's Holy Spirit.

Pro	Con
● Combining promotes unity between kids of different ages.	● Combining makes meeting every person's needs more difficult.
● Some junior and senior highers want to be together.	● Some senior highers resent junior highers' presence; junior highers may feel intimidated by senior highers.
● Many topics span age ranges; for example, friendship, getting along with your family or knowing God.	● Some topics are better fitted to one age group.
● Funds spread farther by combining age groups.	● You may miss the unique challenge of working with one age group.
● More-mature junior high kids may gain more from a combined retreat.	

If you decide to combine your junior highers and senior highers for a retreat, split them for a lock-in at a later date. Then you can focus more on specific age-related needs.

planning, choosing and publicizing. It was *my* retreat, not the *junior highers'* retreat. Because they felt no ownership in the retreat, they didn't show. I should've involved kids in every aspect of the planning.

What other keys contribute to retreat and lock-in success? Couple prayer with planning, love with laughter, Bible study with recreation and affirmation with firm rules.

Key #2: Prayer—Only God can make spiritual growth occur. So saturate every aspect of your event with prayer. Talk with God about each junior higher. Ask for wisdom and energy to meet each junior higher's needs.

Key #3: Planning—Pay attention to every detail, including where you'll stay, what you'll eat, what you'll do during breaks and how you'll handle illness or an emergency. Though detail work sounds unspiritual and boring, it's essential to an event's success. With junior highers coming, always plan more study activities, break ideas and discussion questions than you think you'll need. Then if kids zip through the activity you'd planned for an entire hour, you'll have something to add. Focus your plans on need-meeting activities and themes. Include lots of movement.

The best prevention for discipline problems, boredom, injury and rambunctiousness is a well-planned event.

Key #4: Love—You must genuinely like junior high kids to lose sleep over them, plan with them or bring out the best in them. As you win their trust through loving actions, consistent discipline and need-focused teaching, they'll respond to you and to Jesus Christ.

Key #5: Laughter—When you simply enjoy your time with kids, you communicate love, teach that God is the author of fun, and encourage trust and acceptance. Plan study procedures and break options that encourage Christ-centered fun and sharing.

Key #6: Bible study—None of the other keys have any value unless they're based in scripture. God is the guide for our planning, the source of our love and the reason for our laughter. As you study the Bible with junior highers, keep your methods active, meaningful and practical. During retreats, junior highers can study the Bible on their own with Sealed Orders—a private devotional time when kids each find a secluded spot to commune with God through his Word.

Key #7: Recreation—Notice the "re" in recreation. God can refresh and recreate us through relaxation and fun. Balance study times with recreation, recognizing free time can also teach. Design recreation activities that communicate the theme, build unity in your group, increase kids' confidence and provide opportunities to make new friends.

Key #8: Affirmation—Make certain each retreat or lock-in includes opportunities for concrete expressions of affirmation. Junior highers doubt themselves more persistently than any other age group. Their physical and hormonal changes intensify their concern over how others view them. So give generous amounts of praise and encouragement, and equip kids to affirm each other.

Key #9: Discipline—Junior highers thrive under structure. They push the limits but feel relieved when those limits hold. Remember that discipline means guidance—not punishment. The word "discipline" comes from the same root as "disciple." The goal of all discipline is to teach kids to be self-disciplined. Until junior highers are mature enough to regulate their own behavior, leaders must provide the regulations that give them security.

ANSWERS TO COMMON QUESTIONS

When you take junior high kids on a retreat or host them for a lock-in, you're not just ministering to kids. You're also reaching parents and adult leaders. You minister to parents by helping their kids grow spiritually, providing role models their kids need and giving parents a weekend free of parenting responsibilities. You minister to adult leaders by enabling them to express their spiritual gifts, teaching them to relate to kids and giving them study time.

Take kids', parents' and leaders' questions seriously, answering with as much detail as you have. Inviting questions and responding honestly to them promotes trust.

Especially for retreats, hold a parents' meeting to cover details and answer questions. It takes tremendous trust and confidence for parents to give you the privilege of taking their kids away for an entire weekend. Encourage parents to call you with specific questions.

Brief yourself on these sample questions and answers to hone your skills.

Q: What will my teenager do at the lock-in?
A: Here's a copy of the lock-in schedule. Our lock-in topic is goal-setting. We'll do the bulk of our study early in the evening when the kids are alert. About midnight we'll have a snack and then hold a Table-Games Olympics. We'll sing and worship at about 2:30 a.m. and then sleep from 3 a.m. to 7 a.m. During sleep time, guys will be required to stay in their sleeping room and the girls in theirs. An adult counselor will be with each group. We'll cook, eat breakfast and be ready for departure at about 8 a.m. What other questions do you have?

Q: Why does the retreat cost so much?
A: Factors entering into the cost include retreat site fee—$300 for our group, divided among those who attend; food charge—$7 per person; study materials—$2 per person; and transportation fee—$3 per person. We've tried to keep the cost as low as possible. If you or anyone you know has trouble meeting the cost, let me know and we'll try to find scholarship funds.

Q: Will the kids stay up all night at the lock-in?
A: We'll stay up extremely late but not all night. Staying up all night means we won't be in good shape for the next day's activities.

Q: My daughter comes home all happy from the retreat but the next day she's the same old grump. Is there any way to make the effects last?

A: Your daughter probably encountered God in a new or deeper way. You can help build on this experience in several ways. Notice her joy, compliment it and invite her to tell you about it. Suggest she write God a letter thanking him for the events and experiences of the retreat or lock-in, and telling how she's different because of it. Explain that writing and then rereading helps the joy persist. If she's not a writer, suggest she record her thoughts on a cassette player.

Also invite your daughter to tell you about the people she especially enjoyed on the retreat or lock-in. Offer opportunities to get together with those friends: a sleepover, a church event or lots of phone time.

Finally, encourage your daughter to take time to rest and eat. The physical weariness that usually results from a retreat or lock-in can often lead to emotional distress.

A WRAP-UP

Retreats and lock-ins allow kids time to get away with their peers and examine their hearts, motives, lifestyles and beliefs. Properly done, retreats and lock-ins can be effective tools for growing kids in their understanding and in their relationship with God and each other.

Press on to the following chapters and discover for yourself the excitement and growth possible when you do retreats or lock-ins with junior highers.

Endnotes

[1]Eugene C. Roehlkepartain (editor), *The Youth Ministry Resource Book* (Loveland, CO: Group Books, 1988), 193.

[2]Eugene C. Roehlkepartain (editor), *The Youth Ministry Resource Book* (Loveland, CO: Group Books, 1988), 164.

CHAPTER 2

Planning a Retreat or Lock-In

Good retreats and lock-ins don't just happen. This chapter examines details that create a climate for retreat and lock-in success. Combine God's leadership with the ideas in this chapter to prepare an event that brings lasting spiritual growth in your junior highers.

THE TEN COMMANDMENTS OF RETREATS AND LOCK-INS

Before we launch into the details of planning a junior high retreat or lock-in, let's look at 10 principles that form a foundation on which successful retreats and lock-ins are built. I call these the "Ten Commandments" of successful retreats and lock-ins.

I. Thou shalt keep things moving. Recognize that junior highers learn best when more than their mouths are involved. Notice suggestions in the retreats and lock-ins described in this book that make use of movement, sight, sound, touch, taste and smell.

II. Thou shalt vary activities. Junior high kids—like people of all ages—learn in different ways and at different paces. Rather than worry about which junior higher learns best by which learning style, remember that research shows all kids learn best when learning approaches are varied. That means making use of speaking, writing, drawing, acting, watching, singing, discussing, noticing, creating, listening and more.

III. Thou shalt blend active and quiet learning methods. No one can stand a continuous barrage of active events—nor can anyone endure sitting still for long. Activity provides the experiences that lead to understanding. Quiet events provide reflection on learning, opportunity to commune with God and an atmosphere that encourages sharing.

For example, in Session 1 of the "Dealing With Feelings" retreat, kids bounce balloons with questions about love written on them. That's the experience. Then kids talk about why questions like those on the balloons are always "bouncing" around in our heads. That's the reflection.

IV. Thou shalt include lots of affirmation. Affirmation assures junior highers that they're capable, safe and smart. Affirming them makes it easier for them to believe, accept and live in God's care. Encourage junior highers daily for specific comments or actions you see them say or do.

V. Thou shalt overplan rather than underplan. Overplan so if one activity bombs or takes less time than you expect, you'll have something to do. Junior highers are bright and quick, and may surprise you with how rapidly they absorb and complete assignments.

VI. Thou shalt include adequate supervision. To give kids plenty of attention, affirmation and security, enlist one adult for every six junior highers.

VII. Thou shalt encourage junior highers to participate. Kids learn by doing. Encourage kids to add comments, suggest ideas or get physically involved in the activity. Avoid observation activities except for brief periods. Invite interaction by affirming every contribution and by structuring the activities so each has a part. For example, instead of asking questions of only a few kids, place a question under each person's chair. If kids know everyone will contribute and that their contribution will be accepted, they'll feel more comfortable sharing.

VIII. Thou shalt not hog leadership. No one—not even you—has the energy, time or ability to meet every junior higher's needs. That's why Christ's body is set up the way it is: each person caring for junior highers in the way God has gifted him or her to. Diane's boisterous spirit may intimidate shy kids. But Dan's intense but gentle listening brings out the best in them. Build a team among your leaders through delegation, training and affirmation.

IX. Thou shalt channel kids' energy rather than stifle it. Junior highers exude energy and can usually shift their focus quickly and easily. Variety is the key to keeping kids' interest. Balance an hour of free time with an hour of study time to make the most of kids' energy and time.

Also keep study times active, encouraging kids to use each of their senses. Include activities that highlight seeing, hearing, touching, even tasting. In addition, vary group size by frequently having kids form small groups to discuss a question or do an activity.

X. Thou shalt lead to an effective spiritual climax. Kids need closure. As you plan and lead each element of a retreat or lock-in, arrange the flow to lead toward a spiritual climax. For each part of the event, ask yourself: "How will this activity draw kids closer to God?" "How can this lead to a spiritual turning point?" "How will this impact life rather than just give a good feeling?" "How can this help kids encounter and worship God?"

Close the event with a time of sharing and worship that brings together everything kids have discovered during the retreat or lock-in. Avoid manipulation that encourages empty emotionalism. But lead kids in understanding the implications of what they've learned, and give them time to reflect together on the events they've shared.

FROM START TO FINISH

Planning a retreat or lock-in takes lots of thought, energy and leg-work. At times the details can seem overwhelming—Are there enough beds? Who will do the cooking? Where will the meals be prepared? How do we handle scholarships?

The overall goal of your event can sometimes drown in the mire of details—but not if you plan effectively and give yourself plenty of time to smooth out any rough edges. Let's explore each planning phase you must go through to plan an effective retreat or lock-in.

Choose a date and book a site well in advance. Hop on this one as soon as possible. The best sites book quickly. See the site before you book it, making sure it fits your group's needs. See the "On-Site Checklist" on page 18 to help you decide whether a site's for you. Change sites or dates if one doesn't meet your needs.

Decide your topic and plan the event. How do you choose a topic for your event? Prayerfully consider the following five steps.

1. Identify kids' needs and select a topic that meets one of those needs. For example, if school is about to start, do a retreat on school or friendship. Or if your group is troubled by cliques, lead a lock-in on belonging or self-esteem. Notice both prevention ("They'll be facing school pressures.") and solution ("They're too cliquish!") needs. Never put kids down for their needs. Instead respond sensitively and with God's answers.

2. Identify your own teaching gifts and the gifts of your adult leaders. Do one of you have the ability to talk comfortably and com-

On-Site Checklist

Use this checklist to see how well a potential site fits your group's needs.

❑ **Meeting room size**—How large is your group? What types of teaching activities will you do during the retreat? How well does the space allow for these options?

❑ **Equipment**—What equipment will you use—overhead projectors, film projectors, tape players? Are they available at the site? Is electricity available? How many outlets are there and how conveniently are they located?

❑ **Meals**—Will you prepare your own meals or are they provided by the facility? How much do meals cost? What cooking facilities are available? What type of snacks will they bring? Is refrigeration or freezer space needed?

❑ **Sleeping**—How will guys and girls be divided? Are there enough beds? Avoid settings where two or three kids are "left over" or where guys and girls would have to sleep in the same room.

❑ **Free time**—Do teaching activities require a certain outdoor setting? Are there hiking trails, softball fields and other settings your kids enjoy? What safety rules will be required in this setting? What opportunities for outdoor worship do the grounds provide?

❑ **Cost**—How much does the site cost? Can you afford it? Is choosing this site a demonstration of good stewardship—both of money and learning opportunities?

petently about God's guidelines for sex? Or do you prefer something more like "getting along with parents"? If you have difficulty with a subject, consider bringing in an outside speaker who knows the subject matter and can communicate with kids.

3. Consider the materials you have. This book has step-by-step plans for 12 topics, but you may have extra material on one or more of these topics. Or your kids may request a topic not covered in this book. Can you gather materials to lead it?

4. Notice what your kids show interest in. Distribute a survey listing three or four topics and invite kids to rank them in order of preference. Identify their "felt needs." Your kids may seem more concerned about getting to know God personally than about worship. But because worship contributes to understanding God, it may become an integral part of the retreat. Let the main topic be the one kids are already interested in: knowing God.

5. Strive for balance in your ministry. You may love to teach on loneliness, but have you guided your kids to discover their spiritual gifts?

Determine the event's cost. Retreat costs add up more quickly than lock-in costs, but both can be expensive. Include these expenses in the total cost of the event:

- site fees—note what is and isn't included;
- teaching materials;
- meals and snacks—may include salaries or gifts for the cooks;
- transportation costs;
- adult costs (don't charge leaders—they're already donating their time);
- postage and printing costs;
- insurance fees; and
- speakers' honorariums, if any (the retreats in this book assume you're leading the event).

Use any combination of the following methods to cover the cost:

- Add all the costs and divide by the number of kids you expect. Charge each junior higher this amount.
- Include a portion of the retreat costs in your church's annual budget. Perhaps the church can pay the site and speaker's fees, and the kids pay for the materials, food and transportation.
- Enlist church members or groups to provide scholarships for kids who need them.
- Hold fund-raisers. Decide beforehand whether you'll apply the proceeds only to kids who work in the fund-raiser or to any kids who need the money.

Decide rules as a team. If you resist making rules, remember that rules give the security junior highers crave. These principles tend to make rule-setting and enforcing go more smoothly:

- As you involve your kids in rule-setting, they'll feel more committed to obeying rules.
- Determine rules based on the event's goals, junior high needs, the setting and the topic.

Sample Event Rules

1—Take care of growth. Study hard and play hard by participating in all sessions.

2—Take care of people. Express love for each person: All opinions will be accepted and appreciated by the whole group. No putdowns or criticism allowed.

3—Take care of property. No vandalism or destructive fun—including raiding cabins. No girls in the guys' cabin, no guys in the girls' cabin. Shaving cream fights and other fun events will take place in designated areas at designated times.

Sample Free Time Rules
(For Retreats)

1. Options for free time include:
- ❑ Go to your cabin.
- ❑ Hike in these areas: (list them here).
- ❑ Play volleyball on the recreation field.

2. If you want to do something not on this list, clear it with _____.
(Designate one person for permission-giving so privileges are consistent.)

3. Boundaries are:
- ❑ the road on the north
- ❑ the lake on the south
- ❑ the cabins on the east
- ❑ the eating hall on the west

Do not under any circumstances go beyond these boundaries.

4. No matter what option you choose, let your counselor know your choice. If you change your mind, locate your counselor and indicate your change of plans.

5. These rules are to increase your free time, not restrict it. If we know where you are, we can relax and you can relax.

● Determine two sets of rules: one for the event itself and one for free time. See the "Sample Event Rules" on page 19 and the "Sample Free Time Rules" above.

Where possible, arrange rules in an easy-to-remember form. Some rules are modeled after the Ten Commandments with "Thou shalts" and "Thou shalt nots." Others repeat a phrase or word like the "Sample Event Rules" on page 19. Still others spell something with the first letters of the rules so kids can more easily remember them.

Let junior highers and their parents know the rules ahead of time. This serves several purposes:

● Kids and parents know what to expect and cannot later claim ignorance of the rules.

● You establish a foundation for discipline. When a discipline problem arises during the retreat or lock-in, you have an agreed-upon set of rules to back up your authority.

● Parents can join you in forbidding certain actions such as bringing fireworks, and encouraging others such as bringing Bibles.

● Because kids know the rules ahead of time, they're free to enjoy the retreat or lock-in rather than spend time testing the boundaries.

Decide what result you want and what rules will bring that about. For example, if you want kids to grow closer to each other, set a rule encouraging listening and understanding. If you want spiritual growth through Bible study and worship, set a rule requiring attendance and participation at all sessions.

Write and sign covenants. Work your rules into a covenant junior highers, parents and adult leaders sign before attending the retreat or lock-in. Covenants build trust, communicate with kids and their parents, and encourage personal responsibility. Covenants also minimize hassles and "send-homes" by explaining expectations ahead of time.

Sample Event Covenant

I'm excited about the Christ Church youth retreat (or lock-in). I want to get to know other kids, understand God and myself better, grow spiritually and have fun.

During this event I agree to do the following:

● Treat other kids with respect—not laughing at ideas or answers. This produces an accepting group which in turn gives me the freedom to express my feelings and ideas without fear of ridicule.

● Leave all radios, CD players, stereos and tape players at home. This allows me more time to talk to other kids and God. Because such music is a private type of enjoyment, it can interfere with growing closer to my friends or God. During the event, we'll make our own music or enjoy contemporary Christian music for the entire group.

● Attend all Bible study, worship and organized recreation sessions. This gives me maximum opportunity to understand God and to grow in him.

● Bring no fireworks, alcohol, drugs, people-destroying items or property-destroying items. If caught with these I understand they'll be confiscated and I'll call my parents to tell about the incident. I may be asked to leave the retreat and return home.

● Enjoy myself. This includes seeing the good in people and activities, getting to know people and God, and noticing the beauty of God's handiwork. It also includes having a positive attitude, refraining from pouting, and talking out problems rather than letting them make me grouchy.

● Ask any questions I have, realizing that if it's important enough to wonder or think about, it's important enough to ask about.

_____

Junior higher

I've read and understand this covenant. I'll encourage my junior higher to keep the covenant. Though I anticipate no problems, I'll be available and ready to come get my junior higher if he or she doesn't keep any part of this covenant.

_____

Parent

Menu Ideas

Peruse these ideas to help you choose an event menu that's "just right."

Breakfast

● Breakfast pizza: Make crusts out of canned biscuits and cover with sausage, frozen hash browns, shredded cheeses and other breakfast items. Raw eggs mixed with a little milk form the "sauce." Pour the sauce over the pizza. Bake at 350 degrees for about 30 minutes.

● Weird breakfast: For admission to the event, require kids each to bring "something weird you've eaten for breakfast." Possibilities include cold pizza, leftover spaghetti or hamburgers. Pull these out at 7:00 a.m., heat what needs heating and have a breakfast potluck.

● Carry-in breakfast sandwiches from a restaurant: This is especially handy for lock-ins when everyone's tired.

Other Meals

● Build-your-own pizza: Set pizza crusts with sauce along tables. Provide toppings for kids to create pizzas. Possibilities include: cheese, sausage, hamburger, pepperoni, green pepper, onions, olives, pineapple, tomatoes, mushrooms, ham, shrimp—you name it! Encourage kids to create faces, designs and symbols.

● Sandwich display: Display cold cuts, condiments, bread, chips and cookies. Have kids make sandwiches. If your theme is togetherness, you might give one group the cold cuts, one group the bread and one group the chips. Watch how they share, hoard and barter. Then debrief the experience.

● Order-in pizzas: For lock-ins, have pizza delivered around midnight.

● Hot dogs: Cook these ahead of time and keep them warm in a crock pot. Or roast them over a campfire. Remember to bring buns, condiments, and (if roasting) sticks and marshmallows.

Snacks

● Bring-a-snack: As part of the retreat or lock-in admission, have kids each bring a bag of their favorite chips, cookies or other ready-to-eat snack.

● S'mores: Make this scouting favorite by placing a freshly roasted marshmallow on four squares of a Hershey bar. Then sandwich it between two halves of a graham cracker.

I first began using covenants after two guests created havoc for an entire youth trip. I could've forbidden guests on our next trip, but instead I turned the problem over to our junior highers. They wrote their own covenant for use during future trips. Their wisdom amazed me.

Consider inviting your junior highers to work with you to write a covenant prior to your next event. See the "Sample Event Covenant" on page 21.

Explain the covenant to each junior higher before the retreat or lock-in to lessen the possibility of having to enforce it during the event. Continually remind yourself that junior highers feel secure with reasonable limits—no matter how hard they buck.

If junior highers or their parents refuse to sign, thank them for considering the covenant and tell them you look forward to their participating in other youth program events.

Stand firm even when you fear looking like a meanie, realizing that junior highers take pride in activities that require commitment. Notice ways your junior highers give themselves to band, football practice or play practice—all of which require extensive commitment. Anything of value is worth covenanting for.

Prepare menus and purchase food. Many retreat sites cook your meals and let you provide the snacks. During lock-ins and some retreats, you'll do the cooking yourself. If your retreat site provides meals, be certain the meal cost is figured into your expenses. For retreat or lock-in snack and meal preparation, attend to these details:

● Menus—What will please kids and be nourishing at the same time? What can we afford? What can we store?

● Shopping—Will the person who buys the groceries charge to your church or need to take cash? What limit do you have on cost? Who must approve the menus?

● Food transportation—Will kids bring ingredients or will you bring them yourself?

● Food storage—Does your church have refrigerator space? Can you cook at your church? What refrigeration and cooking facilities are available at the retreat site?

● Cooking—Will adults or kids cook? Who's responsible for seeing that food is ready on time?

Several retreats in this book suggest food ideas that support the theme. For more ideas see the "Menu Ideas" box on page 22. Choose those ideas that best fit your needs.

Plan the games. Games can be as important to your retreat as study times because they can demonstrate the truths you're exploring. Games also help build unity at the beginning of retreats, during transitional times and during structured free time.

Each retreat suggests games that relate to that topic. In addition, feel free to create or discover your own. When selecting or creating games, remember these two guidelines:

1. Select cooperative rather than competitive games, team-focused rather than hero-focused.

2. Reject any games that humiliate, embarrass or confuse any young person or any group of young people.

Scan these classic game ideas to help you work out your own "game plan."

● Organized Shaving Cream Fight—Announce this on the information sheet so kids can each bring a can of shaving cream. Anyone who squirts shaving cream before the fight is disqualified and has his or her shaving cream confiscated. Announce the time and place of the fight. Designate boundaries. Hold the fight right before free time so kids will have time to clean up. Suggest bringing old clothes and a plastic trash bag to carry the clothes home in. Have kids avoid getting shaving cream in others' eyes.

● Killer—Have kids sit in a circle. Give kids each a playing card, one of which is the ace of spades. The one who gets the ace of spades becomes the secret "killer." Have the killer "kill" others by winking at them without anyone else seeing. When someone sees the killer wink at him or her, he or she counts silently to 10, then dramatically "dies" by falling on the floor.

Instruct those who're not yet killed to try to catch the killer winking at someone. Anyone who thinks he or she knows who the killer is should say, "I have an accusation to make. The killer is ____."

Have the "accused" turn over his or her card. If the accused is the killer, re-deal the cards for another round. If not, the accuser is dead and play continues until the killer is caught.

● Board Game Tournament—Invite kids to bring their favorite board games. Bring tournament charts and sign kids up.

● Volleyball—Make it less competitive by playing with a beach ball. Make it more interesting by sitting on the floor to play.

● Non-competitive games and never-before-heard-of games—Find these in sources such as *Quick Crowdbreakers and Games for Youth Groups*, *Group Growers* or *Building Community in Youth Groups* (Group Books).

● Relay races—Invite kids to help you make these up. The possibilities are endless, but here are some examples:

Clothes Exchange—Run to a chair, put on a set of clothes, circle the chair, take off the clothes and run back.

Potato Run—Carry a potato or some other odd object on a spoon as you walk to a point and circle a chair. If the potato falls, begin again.

Crazy Walk—Walk like a crab or move in another unusual position toward a goal. Make the position wild enough to give everyone an equal chance of success. Avoid embarrassing positions.

Obtain consent and liability release forms. Parental consent and release from liability forms help prevent problems before they occur. They provide ways for parents and kids to understand the

Parental Consent Form

Name of event participant _____

Age _____ Birth date _____

Address_____ Phone (____) _____

City _____State_____ZIP_____

School _____Grade in or just completed _____

Parent(s) business phones _____ _____

To whom it may concern:

The undersigned does hereby give permission for our (my) child,

_____, to attend and participate in
(Name of child)

activities sponsored by _____ on _____.
(Church)   (Date)

    We (I) authorize an adult, in whose care the minor has been entrusted, to consent to any X-ray examination, anesthetic, medical, surgical or dental diagnosis or treatment, and hospital care, to be rendered to the minor under the general or special supervision and on the advice of any physician or dentist licensed under the provisions of the Medical Practice Act on the medical staff of a licensed hospital, whether such diagnosis or treatment is rendered at the office of said physician or at said hospital.

    The undersigned shall be liable and agree(s) to pay all costs and expenses incurred in connection with such medical and dental services rendered to the aforementioned child pursuant to this authorization.

    Should it be necessary for our (my) child to return home due to medical reasons or otherwise, the undersigned shall assume all transportation costs.

    The undersigned does also hereby give permission for our (my) child to ride in any vehicle designated by the adult in whose care the minor has been entrusted while attending and participating in activities sponsored by_____.
(Church)

Hospital insurance Yes ❑ No ❑

Insurance company _____

Policy number_____

Emergency phone numbers _____

_____
Church name

_____
Participant   Date

_____
Father   Date

_____
Mother   Date

_____
Legal guardian   Date

On the reverse side of this page, please list any allergies or special medical problems your child may have. Thank you.

Liability Release Form

Release of All Claims

In consideration for being accepted by _____

(Church name)

for participation in _____,

(Name of trip or activity)

we (I), being 21 years of age or older, do for ourselves (myself) [and for and on behalf of our (my) child-participant if said child is not 21 years of age or older] hereby release, forever discharge and agree to hold harmless

_____and the directors thereof from

(Church name)

any and all liability, claims or demands for personal injury, sickness or death, as well as property damage and expenses, of any nature whatsoever which may be incurred by the undersigned and the child-participant that occur while said child is participating in the above-described trip or activity.

Furthermore, we (I) [and on behalf of our (my) child-participant if under the age of 21 years] hereby assume all risk of personal injury, sickness, death, damage and expense as a result of participation in recreation and work activities involved therein.

Further, authorization and permission is hereby given to said church to furnish any necessary transportation, food and lodging for this participant.

The undersigned further hereby agree(s) to hold harmless and indemnify said church, its directors, employees and agents, for any liability sustained by said church as the result of the negligent, willful or intentional acts of said participant, including expenses incurred attendant thereto.

(If the participant has not attained the age of 21 years):
We (I) are the parent(s) or legal guardian(s) of this participant, and hereby grant our (my) permission for him (her) to participate fully in said trip, and hereby give our (my) permission to take said participant to a doctor or hospital and hereby authorize medical treatment, including but not in limitation to emergency surgery or medical treatment, and assume the responsibility of all medical bills, if any.

continued

Further, should it be necessary for the participant to return home due to medical reasons, disciplinary action or otherwise, we (I) hereby assume all transportation costs.

_____
(Type or print name of participant)

(Only participant need sign if 21 years of age or older. If under 21, both parents must sign unless parents are separated or divorced in which case the custodial parent must sign.)

_____
(Parent's telephone)

_____
(Pastor's telephone)

_____   _____
Father   Date

Hospital insurance   Yes ❑   No ❑
Insurance company

_____

_____   _____
Mother   Date

Policy number_____

Physician _____

Physician's phone _____

_____   _____
Legal guardian   Date

Emergency phone numbers _____

_____

_____   _____
Participant, if age 21   Date

Trip Participant Only

I have read the foregoing and understand the rules of conduct for participants and will abide by them as well as the directions of the leadership of the trip.

_____
Participant

retreat or lock-in and recognize their responsibilities in it. They also save valuable time in case of a medical emergency. Ultimately, they are an expression of trust between you and parents.

Here's an overview of each form's purpose:

● Parental consent form—This form assures you that the young person's parent or guardian wants him or her to attend the event. It also authorizes adults at the event to approve medical treatment required in an emergency. See the "Parental Consent Form" on page 25.

● Liability release form—You can use this form to help build your case in the event of a liability suit. Although the form doesn't provide blanket protection, it can be used as favorable evidence in court. See the "Liability Release Form" on page 26.

Event Checklist

Check off each item as you complete it.
❑ Choose a date.
❑ Book a site.
❑ Decide on your topic.
❑ Design the program.
❑ Determine the event's cost.
❑ Decide rules as a team.
❑ Write and sign covenants.
❑ Prepare menus and purchase food.
❑ Plan the games.
❑ Obtain consent and liability release forms.

Are the forms too much hassle? Not at all. Actually, they prevent hassles with kids and their parents.

Prepare and distribute these forms in a packet along with these other important materials:

● a general information sheet explaining departure time and location, event address and phone, what to bring and other important information; and

● a copy of the covenant written by your group for this event.

Instruct junior highers to keep the information sheet but to sign and return the other three forms to you. Leave the "Liability Release Forms" at your church, but take the "Parental Consent Forms" with you in case of a medical emergency.

UPON ARRIVAL

As kids arrive at a lock-in or retreat, provide an arrival activity so they don't stand around wondering what to do. Possibilities include:
  ● a challenge related to your study (see lock-in and retreat plans for ideas);

Getting Into Groups

As you study, you'll want to gather your kids for discussion, response and spiritual growth. Consider the pros and cons of these four options.

One Group in a Circle
  ● This allows for circular response with everyone adding something.
  ● Circle groups make everyone feel at home and equally important.

Small Groups
Lots of possibilities here; for example:
  ● Keep kids with the same small group the whole weekend. This encourages accountability, closeness and trust-building, but limits contact to these few.
  ● Keep kids in the same group for one session only. This enables them to get to know many people, but limits continuation of previous discussion and forces kids to start all over in developing trust.
  ● Let kids choose their groups. Choosing encourages responsible choice-making but may result in kids staying with their friends rather than branching out.
  ● Designate the groups yourself. This enables you to split up destructive chemistry, but you may unintentionally arrange a bad match.

Pairs
  ● Pairs increase the probability that all kids will work on the assignment rather than one or two in a small group completing it while everyone else watches.
  ● Pairs encourage friendship and trust without competition.
  ● Pairs mean someone may be left without a partner. Form a threesome or work with the "extra" junior higher yourself.

Individual Work
  ● This is especially effective for morning devotions.
  ● Some junior highers have trouble staying on a task when working alone. Others feel more secure when no one is watching and thus do better.

Vary the options to take advantage of each. For example, if you keep the same study groups throughout the retreat, use different groups for worship sessions. Or use one large group to begin and end sessions but pairs or small groups between.

● a beach ball volleyball game or another game kids can easily join; or

● a scavenger hunt you set up beforehand.

When everyone has arrived, gather kids in a quiet spot and go over these details:

● Encourage kids to let their actions glorify God. Read aloud Colossians 3:23 or 1 Corinthians 10:31.

● Encourage kids to treat the people and property with respect.

● Tell kids to bring their Bibles to every meeting.

● Review your rules, encouraging kids to recite them.

● Pray as a group for God's guidance.

● Instruct kids to unpack, get settled and report to the central meeting room in 20 minutes. Say that early arrivers will receive a bonus but don't tell what it is. Candy works well, but avoid gum. Tell kids that if anyone is late, the entire group will be penalized.

UPON DEPARTURE

If your group's like most, it can trash a site within seconds. Deal with this difficulty by inviting kids to use that same energy to clean up. Don't allow anyone to leave a room after a meeting until:

● all trash is in the trash can;

● all pencils are in the pencil box; and

● all Bibles are on the Bible table.

When you leave the retreat site, follow a similar procedure, assigning kids to different areas. For example:

● girls clean up girls' cabin;

● guys clean up guys' cabin;

● everyone walks side by side through the retreat site picking up any trash.

AFTER THE EVENT

It's over!

But how'd it go? Did the kids grow spiritually? What impact will the retreat or lock-in have on their lives? Though only God knows the event's full impact, evaluation can help you plan more effectively for the next retreat or lock-in. Mix and match these ideas to involve junior highers and their leaders in evaluating the retreat:

● Invite each junior higher to write down the best and worst of the retreat or lock-in.

● Invite each leader to write a paragraph about the junior higher who grew most dramatically and how.

● Guide the entire group to evaluate the retreat or lock-in using one or more of the following open-ended statements. Record kids' responses on large paper or an overhead transparency.

1. During this event, I discovered that God ...

2. The best part of the event was ...

3. The worst part of the event was ...

4. On a scale of 1 to 10 (10=super) I'd rate this event as a __ because ...

5. If I could omit something on the next event, it'd be ...

6. The person who helped me grow the most on this event was _____ because ...

7. My life will be different now because ...

● Evaluate two times: once on the last day of the event and once a month later. Vary the evaluation method you use.

● ● ●

Seems like a lot of information to take in, doesn't it? Even though there are many steps in planning an effective retreat or lock-in, caring for the details will become more automatic after you've involved your group in a few events like this. Just remember to use checklists wherever possible and to delegate as much planning as you can. That way you'll cover details more efficiently and build teamwork at the same time.

As you plan your first retreat or lock-in, refer to this chapter and the checklist on page 28. Go through each section of this chapter to be sure you've taken care of every detail. Check back with people you've delegated responsibility to. And, of course, saturate everything you do in prayer. Doing all of these will help ensure your event's success—both in your kids' eyes as well as God's.

CHAPTER 3

Training Workers for Retreats and Lock-Ins

Two months before a scheduled lock-in, the youth council met and decided they wanted to study friendship. They felt friendship problems were destroying their youth group. So they wrote specific examples, changing each so they wouldn't identify anyone involved. Then they gave the situations to their youth leader.

They suggested three possible dates for the lock-in, brainstormed possibilities for adults they'd like along and prayed for God's guidance. The youth leader took their information, checked the church calendar and selected a date. She then enlisted adult leaders; prepared consent forms, liability forms and covenants; found materials to guide the retreat; and trained leaders. Together with the youth council, she publicized the lock-in and signed up kids. Parents were enlisted to pray, cook and attend the lock-in.

The lock-in was a great success. Many kids came and participated in the sessions. Sharing was genuine and supportive. The kids addressed real problems with scripture and prayer. All left feeling closer than they had in years.

An ideal story? Certainly—but one worth working toward. Notice the three sets of people crucial to making a junior high retreat or lock-in work:

- junior highers;
- adult leaders—including you; and
- parents.

When all these work together, retreats and lock-ins can become life-changing experiences. Of course you may encounter a few uncooperative teenagers, struggle to get enough counselors to go along or talk to parents who're more interested in getting rid of their junior highers for a weekend than in seeing them grow spiritually. But you can minimize these problems through:

- training adult leaders;
- training junior highers; and
- communicating with parents and kids.

TRAINING ADULT LEADERS

When you enlist adult leaders, affirm them by explaining why you chose them: "I've watched the way you talk with junior highers in the hall—you show such genuine love for them. I think both they and you would enjoy your going on our event."

Continue by explaining what's expected of them at the retreat or lock-in. Resist the temptation to say, "There's nothing to it!" There *is* something to leading youth retreats and lock-ins. When adult sponsors understand what's expected of them, they're more likely to do it. For example, you might say: "I'd like you to be responsible for a group of six girls. This means you'll take special interest in them, sleep in their cabin with them, share devotional time with them and encourage them to grow in Christ. I'll provide training to help you do this, and I have all the materials you need. We leave Friday the 23rd about 6 p.m. and we'll be back Sunday morning the 25th by the close of morning worship."

Show your potential leader the teenage covenant you plan to use and a leader covenant you'd like them to agree to. See the "Sample Leader Covenant" on page 34 for ideas on how to draw up your own leader covenant.

Invite questions. Encourage the potential leader to pray about the decision. Then call him or her after a few days.

Covering the issues—Gather your recruited leaders for training a month or so before the retreat or lock-in. If one or more are unable to attend, get with them individually. Include in your training:
- overview of the event;
- overview of junior high needs and goals for this event;
- explanation of their role as leaders;
- step-by-step guide through each session;
- instruction for cabin or small group devotions;
- ways to encourage spiritual growth in junior highers;
- instruction on leading discussions (see "Discussion Dos and Don'ts" on page 35);
- examination of the rules and ways to enforce them; and
- plenty of time for questions.

Dealing with discipline—Assure leaders that though junior highers often buck discipline, they greatly appreciate it. For example, when leaders insist that junior highers attend each session, kids can freely participate without feeling stupid in front of their friends—"We have to go because the leader said so." Emphasize that rules free junior highers to enjoy themselves and each other.

Sample Leader Covenant

As an adult helper I have the opportunity to help our junior highers grow spiritually, emotionally and socially. Six teenagers will be my personal responsibility. However, my ministry will certainly go beyond these six.

Learning—Participate in all sessions with the kids, first making sure all my group members are there. Prior to the retreat, attend all planning sessions unless providentially hindered.

Encouragement—Give each teenager genuine compliments and avoid any hint of a putdown. Promote unity in the group by affirming members and making all visitors and members feel welcome.

Attentiveness—Know where my assigned junior highers are and what they're doing.

Devotions—Lead devotions with my group members each night. The youth leader will provide materials and show how to use them.

Example of Christ—Cultivate a Christlike attitude at all times. Do what I think Jesus would do in each situation I encounter.

Rules—Obey the rules myself and motivate junior highers to obey them. Help kids understand the retreat rules as ways to increase their fun, not ruin it. If I don't understand the reason for a rule, I'll ask.

I understand my responsibilities and will complete them with God as my guide.

_____

Adult worker

As you discuss discipline with your volunteers, cover these issues:

● Discipline means guidance, not punishment. The extreme energy and enthusiasm of junior highers almost always requires discipline. Discipline works best when junior highers themselves help set and enforce the rules.

● No matter how thoroughly you plan in order to prevent discipline problems, they still come up. Recognize most of these as tests to see how firmly you'll hold to the rules or as indicators of kids' unmet needs.

● When kids do test the limits, remember that junior highers find security in rules. Hold firm no matter how much they fight you, reminding yourself that firm guidelines bring out the best in junior highers. Ideally, the kids will have helped you set the rules and you can remind them of their contribution. Also, clearly explain the reasons for rules and their consequences. Understanding breeds cooperation.

Discussion Dos and Don'ts

Use your actions and attitudes to invite every kid to participate. Try these dos and don'ts, remembering that junior highers' self-esteem and relationship with God are more important than their active participation.

Do:
● Affirm every comment.
● Use questions and comments such as "What do the rest of you think?" or "Good comment. Who has something to add?"
● Provide safe ways for everyone to respond. For example, "Each of us will add an idea and I'll write them all down. Then we'll summarize."
● Give warning of what you'll ask. For example, "In a minute, I'll ask each of you to share a way to make friends that begins with the first letter of your first name."
● Tell kids where they can find answers. For example, "The answers to these questions are in Matthew 18."
● Focus on concrete answers. Facts and specifics are easier for junior highers to identify than attitudes or abstract principles.

Don't:
● Put kids down. An off-the-wall comment may be a test to see how you'll respond. Instead of rejecting the comment, say, "That's not exactly what I expected; would you like to try again?"
● Say, "Why don't you ever talk?" Instead, provide safe ways to respond. For example, place a question under every chair or have an "open book" test with kids checking a Bible passage for answers.
● Allow other kids to talk while one person is sharing. Instead, encourage kids to have the same respect for others that they would want for themselves.

● When kids disobey because they have an unmet need, work to discover the need and meet it. For example, if a disruptive teenager is hunting for attention, help him or her find ways to get attention positively. Have him or her set up the room with you or write kids' responses on newsprint during a discussion.

Other needs that may motivate kids to cause problems include the need for security, the need to belong, the need to "look smart," the need for understanding and the need for friendship.

For each discipline problem that arises, consider these options.

● Give consequences that match the offense. For example, if a teenager comes late to a study session, keep him or her late to the next free time session. If possible, announce consequences ahead of time in the covenant or through the list of rules. For example, include a rule such as "If you leave the designated area, you'll be 'hand-cuffed' to a leader the rest of the day."

● Confiscate contraband items, such as radios, CD players, alcohol, drugs or fireworks. Return radios and CD players after the event. Turn fireworks over to the teenager's parents. Follow your church leaders' guidance concerning alcohol and drug problems.

● Talk privately with the problem teenager. For example, say: "Tracy, I need your help. You've been telling jokes and laughing at other kids when they contribute to discussion. Because they value your opinion, I need you to say something positive for everything they say. It'll build group unity. Will you do that for me?"

● Deny privileges such as free time or snacks to kids who break rules.

● Always affirm good behavior.

Decide also what merits sending a junior higher home. Note that parents agree on the covenant to come get their teenager if necessary. A teenager may need to be sent home when he or she:

● after warnings, continues to disrupt everyone else's learning with little evidence of a behavior change;

● is seriously ill;

● has a drug or alcohol problem; or

● displays inappropriate sexual behavior with other group members.

But before sending a teenager home, consider:

● This may be his or her only chance for spiritual training.

● He or she may change before the event is over.

● The home may be the source of the teenager's problems.

TRAINING JUNIOR HIGHERS

Rather than "putting on a show" for your junior highers, develop their leadership potential by guiding them to help plan, promote and lead the event.

Giving leadership to junior highers means inviting them to join the team—not giving them full control. Even adults have difficulty handling leadership that's simply placed in their laps. Train your youth leaders gradually, giving them more responsibility as they succeed. Always include these four checkpoints:

1. Clarify the assignment. Explain what's required and how to do it. For example, if you ask a few kids to plan the free time, give them books they can choose activities from. Encourage them to choose more activities than they think they'll need in case one bombs. Also, explain their time limits and emphasize that the activities need to be safe and inclusive of everyone.

2. Check kids' progress. Explain ahead of time that all plans will be fine-tuned with the help of an adult leader. Ask questions such as: "What are the strengths and shortcomings of this activity?" "What equipment is needed?" "How long will it take?" "What's 'Plan B'?"

3. Make a checklist for kids to complete. Help kids remember details by having them complete a checklist you design. Remember, you're ultimately responsible for the event. Don't give kids full responsibility for any activity. Instead, encourage junior highers to take responsibility with you and minimize their possibility of failure.

4. After the activity, evaluate the results. Affirm success. Look for ways the activity can be done better next time. For example, a junior higher who chose volleyball as a midday activity might've been wiser to have chosen water volleyball since the weather was hot and a pool was available. Or perhaps the leader should've split teams according to birth dates rather than guys vs. girls. However the evaluation goes, be sure to praise your kids for their efforts.

When you're specific with instructions, persistent with follow-through and generous with praise, junior highers can lead beautifully. Examine these ways kids can work as leaders at a retreat or lock-in.

Food—Everyone eats meals and snacks during a retreat or lock-in. Let teenagers help with this important part of the event by:
- planning menus;
- purchasing food—provide guidelines for how much is needed;
- preparing food; or
- organizing cleanup—have kids prepare a chart with everyone's name and a rotation of responsibilities.

Worship—Encountering God is the central reason for lock-ins and retreats. Junior highers have good ideas for helping this happen. Have your junior high leaders:
- choose songs;
- lead singing; or
- share testimonies—provide a specific topic such as how Jesus improves friendships.

Study time—Study sessions enable junior highers to discover for themselves how to apply the Bible to their lives. Study also provides opportunities for junior highers to learn from each other and build relationships. Encourage your junior high leaders to help in study time by:
- leading small groups—train junior high leaders to lead effective discussions;

● choosing the topic—let kids decide on the retreat or lock-in study topic; or

● leading part of the study—give junior highers limited portions of content to present, explaining specifically how to do so.

Group-building—Closeness comes through shared experiences. Especially since junior highers are prone to embarrassment and self-consciousness, let them choose the types of experiences they would most enjoy. For example, kids can:

● choose games—provide books junior highers can pull games from to play at the event; or

● act as care-givers—kids who're designated to watch for opportunities to build unity, such as including everyone, sitting by a loner or complimenting someone.

PREVENTING DISASTER

Many say experience is the best teacher, but you don't have to encounter every problem to learn how to prevent it. Read the following problems and consider the advice that follows each one. Notice actions and attitudes that could've prevented each of the problems. Then review your ministry problems and consider actions that might prevent them in the future.

Problem: On our last lock-in, my adult leaders were as much trouble as the kids. They led water balloon fights in a Sunday school classroom and refused to discipline the kids. They talked during meetings and slept in rather than attending the morning sessions.

Advice: Leaders, like junior highers, need to know what's expected of them before they attend a lock-in. What may be obvious to you may never dawn on chaperones. Prior to the event, meet with your adult leaders and go over a covenant of responsibilities. Be positive, emphasizing the ministry possibilities of each expectation. Invite adult leaders to read the covenant, ask questions and then sign it. Give them each a copy of the covenant to keep.

Also recognize that different volunteers may have different responsibilities during different events. For some events the cook may have little interaction with kids, sleeping separately so he or she can rest before cooking breakfast. During other events the cook may supervise a group of junior highers in preparing meals all weekend. Consider these questions when preparing a leadership covenant.

● How do you expect leaders to help with study time? Do you want them to find and gather all junior highers before they sit down for a meeting? Do you want them to lead discussion groups?

● How do you expect volunteers to help during free time? Do you want them to play organized sports with the junior highers or just oversee the events?

● What rules do you expect volunteers to enforce? Which rules would you rather deal with yourself?

● What ways do you want the leaders to help kids grow spiritually, emotionally or socially?

Problem: My junior highers trash every room they enter. I'm convinced they have the ability to multiply debris. It takes me as long to clean up after them as to teach the session!

Advice: Consideration for the retreat or lock-in site can be as important as the sessions themselves. Junior highers grow by taking responsibility. Cleanup can help kids feel like part of the body, take pride in their efforts and recognize that no one has to do much dirty work when everyone works together.

Insist that no junior higher or adult leave a room until all paper is in the trash can, all pencils are in the pencil box and all chairs are arranged for the next session. Junior highers may groan and fuss but they'll follow through. And it doesn't hurt to remind them that the more time they spend cleaning up, the less time they'll have for recreation.

Problem: Some of my best adult leaders have junior high children in our group. I'm not sure it's wise to have parents as volunteers.

Advice: Ask the junior higher. Many don't mind their parents being along at all. Others will agree to a parent's presence if the parent doesn't sleep in the same cabin. Still others are inhibited by their parent's presence. Quality retreat or lock-in leadership depends more on personality and spiritual giftedness than whose parent the person is.

Will the parent minister to all junior highers or dote on his or her junior higher? Will the parent allow his or her teenager freedom to share? Will the parent expect more or less of his or her teenager? Notice that some parents bring out the best in their teenagers while others create problems. Talk with both the junior higher and the parent to assess the dynamics between them and decide the best option.

SECTION 2:

Junior High Retreats

Liking Myself So I Can Like You

We've been taught repeatedly that the way to live the Christian life is to put God first, others second and ourselves third. Starting with self-love sounds backward and selfish. But Jesus commanded us, " 'Love your neighbor as [you love] yourself' " (Matthew 22:39b). The way we feel about ourselves directly affects the way we treat others.

To truly love others we must be comfortable with ourselves—so that we can forget ourselves and reach out to others. This begins by learning to accept God's acceptance of us. As we love and accept ourselves the way God does, we can love without walls or conditions.

OBJECTIVES

During this retreat junior highers will:
- define self-esteem and its importance;
- discover biblical truths about their self-worth;
- have an opportunity to accept love;
- discover ways to respond to embarrassment; and
- build self-esteem.

SUPPLY CHECKLIST

You'll need:
- ❑ 3×5 cards
- ❑ bandanna
- ❑ scissors
- ❑ tape
- ❑ newsprint
- ❑ marker
- ❑ one yard of fake fur
- ❑ hot dog meal with all the trimmings

For each group of three or four you'll need:
- ❑ "Nature Hunt List" handout (page 52)

For each person you'll need:
- ❑ lump of clay or pipe cleaner
- ❑ Bible
- ❑ pencil
- ❑ two envelopes
- ❑ tin can
- ❑ "I Was So Embarrassed!" handout (page 50)
- ❑ "Me Booklet" handout (page 54)

RETREAT PREPARATION

● **Face the Facts**—Write each word of the following sentence on a separate 3×5 card and scramble the order: Self-esteem is loving yourself the way God loves you. Provide one complete set of words for every four to six kids.

● **Bring-Along Snack**—Instruct kids each to bring a snack such as chips, fruit or cookies. Supply water, ice and cups.

● **Saturday's Sealed Orders**—Prepare kids each an envelope with these instructions inside: "Read 1 John 4:7-12 and write on the back of this paper the two phrases you find most powerful and the two questions you most want to ask."

● **Spell Out Acceptance**—Divide a piece of paper into 10 sections. In each section write one letter from the word "self-esteem." Make enough copies so each junior higher gets one letter. Cut apart the letters.

● **Embarrassment Relief**—Pick an outgoing teenager to act out the part of Eutychus in the story from Acts 20:7-12. Brief the teenager on what you'll do and give him or her time to prepare.

● **I Can Love Myself**—"Me Booklet" for each person. Photocopy pages 54 and 55. Then place them back to back and tape them together. Or photocopy them on the front and back of the same page. Then fold them down the middle to create the booklet.

● **Theme Snack**—Prepare hot dogs with all the trimmings for each junior higher.

● **Sunday's Sealed Orders**—Prepare kids each an envelope containing these instructions: "In your Bible, underline the phrase in Psalm 139:13-18 that means the most to you. Now on the paper write that phrase in your own words, illustrate it or draw an example of how to live it."

● **Closing Worship**—Create "warm fuzzies" by cutting fake fur into small squares. Make enough so each teenager can have five.

ON THE ROAD

Because talking and sharing about yourself builds self-esteem, give each member an opportunity to talk with every other member. In the bus or van, first have junior highers sit in alphabetical order and direct them each to share their name, their school's name and their best- and worst-liked subjects.

Then have kids arrange themselves by birthdays and have them each tell about their best and worst birthday. Also have them each tell about their "dream" birthday.

Next, have kids arrange themselves by hair color—lightest to darkest—and talk about what they like and don't like about their hair. Tell them they must each say one positive comment for every negative comment.

Finally, have kids each sit with someone they haven't sat with yet and talk about what they hope will happen on this retreat.

If you have time, rearrange the kids again and cover these topics:
● what I like to do in my free time;
● what I like to read;
● the last movie I saw; and
● what I'd like to be in 10 years.

THE RETREAT

FRIDAY

SESSION 1: I LOVE GOD TO BUILD MY ESTEEM

The Shape of Acceptance—As junior highers enter, give each a lump of clay or a pipe cleaner. Say: **Shape this into something people at your school use to gain acceptance.**

Have junior highers show their sculptures one at a time. Generously praise each by explaining why it's right. For example, "Your money sculpture is insightful because people tend to rank rich people as instantly acceptable." Or "Clothing is an excellent example of acceptance-seeking. Some people don't feel right if they don't wear the right labels."

Ask:
● **Which of these acceptance sources do you tend to depend on?**
● **What is the weakness in each?**
● **Is there any source of acceptance that always works? Explain.**

Face the Facts—Form teams of four to six. Give each team a set of scrambled cards containing words from the sentence: Self-esteem is loving yourself the way God loves you.

Challenge teams to unscramble the sentence.

After teams finish, ask:
● **How else might you define self-esteem?**

RETREAT SCHEDULE

FRIDAY

8 p.m.	Session 1: I Love God to Build My Esteem
9:30 p.m.	Welcome and Rule Reminders
9:45 p.m.	Bring-Along Snack
10 p.m.	Smaug's Jewels
11 p.m.	Cabin Devotions: Believing the Truth

SATURDAY

8 a.m.	Breakfast
8:30 a.m.	Sealed Orders
9 a.m.	Session 2: I Love You to Build Your Esteem
10:30 a.m.	Free Time
Noon	Lunch
1 p.m.	Session 3: I Work Through Embarrassment to Build Esteem
3 p.m.	Free Time
4:30 p.m.	Nature Hunt
5:30 p.m.	Clean Up for Supper
6 p.m.	Supper
7 p.m.	Session 4: I Love Me to Build My Esteem
8:30 p.m.	Theme Snack
9 p.m.	Games
10 p.m.	Cabin Devotions: Overcoming the Barriers

SUNDAY

8 a.m.	Breakfast
8:30 a.m.	Sealed Orders
9 a.m.	Closing Worship
10 a.m.	Take Off!

● **Is being conceited the same thing as liking yourself? Explain.**

● **How can you tell conceited people from people who simply like themselves?**

Say: **Appropriate self-love frees me to turn outside myself to love others. Until I accept myself, I'll be consumed with getting others to like me.**

Give each person a Bible. Guide junior highers to memorize Ephesians 2:10 by having them read it aloud in unison. After a couple of repetitions, have someone start a rap rhythm. Help kids set the words to that rhythm. Have fun with it. After several repetitions, call for volunteers to recite the verse from memory.

Ask:

● **How do you feel about being handcrafted by God?**

● **How does this verse change the way you see yourself?**

● **How does this verse change what you do or think?**

God Made Me Good—Sing "God Is So Good" using verses like "God made me good," "I'm his handiwork" and "God made __(name)__ good."

Say: **Through Jesus, God has made us good, but we have to accept and live our God-given goodness.**

Invite kids to receive God's love by becoming a Christian or reaffirming their faith in Jesus Christ.

WELCOME AND RULE REMINDERS

Welcome the group. Share how glad you are each individual came and how important everyone is to the retreat.

Review rules by inviting kids and sponsors to share their dreams for the retreat. Point out how the rules can help each of these dreams happen.

BRING-ALONG SNACK

Set out the snacks kids brought along as part of their retreat supplies. Supplement with any you brought. Serve kids ice water. Circulate and enjoy talking as you and kids eat.

SMAUG'S JEWELS

Play Smaug's Jewels from *The New Games Book* by New Games Foundation (Doubleday/Dolphin). One person plays Smaug. Smaug stays on all fours and is responsible for keeping anyone from stealing the jewels—a knotted bandanna. Smaug's touch instantly paralyzes a would-be thief until the end of the game. Once the jewels are stolen, the thief becomes Smaug.

After the game, ask:

● **How do we try to protect our jewel of self-esteem?**

● **How might we "paralyze" or alienate people in the process?**

● **What better alternatives do we have?**

CABIN DEVOTIONS: BELIEVING THE TRUTH

After kids get into their bunks, have the cabin leader read aloud Ephesians 2:10 and Genesis 1:26-27, 31.

Ask:

● **On a scale of 1 to 10—10 being "super easy"—how easy is it to believe these verses? Why?**

● **What actions or attitudes can help you live out these verses?**

● **How can we help each other believe in our God-given worth?**

SATURDAY

SEALED ORDERS

Send kids each outside with their Bible, pencil and an envelope containing their "Sealed Orders." Allow about 10 minutes.

When kids return, invite them to share their phrases and questions. Involve kids in answering each other's questions about the phrases.

SESSION 2: I LOVE YOU TO BUILD YOUR ESTEEM

Spell Out Acceptance—As junior highers enter, give each a piece of paper with a letter from "self-esteem" and say: **Write on your letter one way to build another's self-esteem.**

Have kids report their ideas and tape their letters to the floor, wall or ceiling to spell self-esteem. Use extra letters to make complete words.

Show Your Faith—Form pairs. Give each pair paper and a pencil. Challenge pairs each to list more esteem-building actions than any other pair. Have them read aloud in unison 1 John 4:7-12 to give them ideas. Allow 90 seconds.

When time is up, have pairs read their lists. Then say: **The actions you've listed are all ways to show our love for God. The nice side effect is that they build up others' self-esteem.**

Bring Out the Good in Someone—Say: **Often we worry so much about our own self-esteem that we forget we affect other people's self-esteem.**

Invite kids to list a few self-esteem crushers they've used. Distribute tin cans and instruct kids each to stomp their can each time someone names a self-esteem crusher. Write the self-esteem crushers on newsprint as kids share.

After a few minutes, have kids display their cans. Challenge kids to make the cans whole and unwrinkled again.

Ask:

● **Which is easier: to repair the can or restore another person's self-esteem? Explain.**

● **How do you feel when someone says a self-esteem crusher to you or about you?**

● **What might give us the courage to build up rather than tear down?**

Say: **You can put an end to one corner of cruelty. You can build somebody up rather than smash their self-esteem.**

Have junior highers each choose a self-esteem crusher and translate it into a self-esteem creator. For example, kids could say "Good to see you" instead of "Why did *you* come?"

99-Second Love—Give each person paper and a pencil. Say: **On "go," you'll have 99 seconds to write the names of everyone you can think of along with words you can say to them to build their self-esteem. At least half the people you list must be at this retreat. Write fast and furiously. Neatness doesn't count. Go!**

After 99 seconds, say: **Now fold your self-esteem-building sheets, write your name on the outside and give them to me. I won't read them, but I'll give them back at the end of the retreat. See how many of the listed words you can say by then.**

Close with prayer.

SESSION 3: I WORK THROUGH EMBARRASSMENT TO BUILD ESTEEM

My Most Embarrassing Moment—As junior highers enter, give them each a pencil and an "I Was So Embarrassed!" handout, and have them complete it.

When everyone is finished, form groups of four and have kids share their responses within their groups.

After groups finish, call everyone together and ask:

● **What things embarrassed you?**

● **What do you do when you get embarrassed?**

● **How does it help to know that other people get embarrassed too?**

● **What does God want us to do when we get embarrassed?**

Read aloud Hebrews 4:15-16. Say: **This passage explains that Jesus can sympathize with us and wants us to approach him confidently in times of need.**

Ask:

● **What do we need when we're embarrassed?**

Say: **Jesus cares about our embarrassing moments as well**

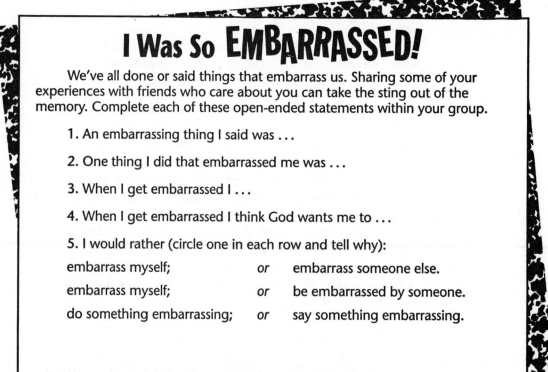

I Was So EMBARRASSED!

We've all done or said things that embarrass us. Sharing some of your experiences with friends who care about you can take the sting out of the memory. Complete each of these open-ended statements within your group.

1. An embarrassing thing I said was . . .

2. One thing I did that embarrassed me was . . .

3. When I get embarrassed I . . .

4. When I get embarrassed I think God wants me to . . .

5. I would rather (circle one in each row and tell why):

embarrass myself;	or	embarrass someone else.
embarrass myself;	or	be embarrassed by someone.
do something embarrassing;	or	say something embarrassing.

as ones that seem more "spiritual." He wants to help us fix our blunders and make the most of our embarrassing experiences.

Embarrassment Relief—Tell the story of Eutychus falling out of the window in Acts 20:7-12. Have the teenager you picked ahead of time act out the passage while you read it.

After the reading, ask:
- **How do you think Eutychus felt after it was all over?**
- **How did Paul feel?**
- **Do you think Eutychus went back to the service? Why or why not?**

Say: **We can help each other through embarrassing moments. Open your Bibles to Ephesians 4:1-6. Each of you choose a phrase you think would help someone who feels embarrassed.**

Encourage each junior higher to choose a different phrase until all the phrases have been chosen. If your group is small, give each person several turns. If your group is large, ask people each to give a different example when they pick the same phrase.

Turn Embarrassment Into Good—Encourage young people each to share one thing they learned or one way they grew through an embarrassing moment. Say: **God won't let bad things spoil his good plans for us. He can take the bad and transform it into some sort of good results. Let him do that in your life.**

Invite kids each to apply their phrase from Ephesians 4:1-6 aloud like this: "To ease my own embarrassment or the embarrassment of a friend I will ..."

NATURE HUNT

Call everyone together. Form teams of three to four. Give each team a "Nature Hunt List." Direct teams each to find the items on the list before any other team. Teams must stay together to find each item. Vary the items on the list to match your setting.

SESSION 4: I LOVE ME TO BUILD MY ESTEEM

God Made Me Good—As junior highers enter, repeat the "God made me good" choruses you sang at the end of the first session.

I Can Love Myself—Give each junior higher a pencil and a "Me Booklet."

Have kids find a comfortable spot and fill out the first page. After a few minutes call for volunteers to share the verse they chose and explain why they chose it. Then have volunteers read their verse with their names inserted.

Have kids each move on to page two and complete it. After a few minutes, invite volunteers to share items from their lists.

Ask:

● **How easy was it to write good things about yourself? Why?**
● **Who has some blank spaces we can help fill up?**

Invite kids and adult teachers to suggest good things to specific kids to fill in their blank spaces.

Now move on to page three and say: **The book of 1 John teaches that loving others shows that God is in you. Jesus himself said to love others as you love yourself. List ways you can think of to love same-age friends, older friends and younger friends.**

After several minutes call on volunteers to share one of their answers. Encourage kids to act on what they've written.

Say: **Pass your booklets one person to the left.**

After kids have passed their booklets, say: **Sign page four of the booklet you now have to indicate that you love that person. You may also write a brief message if you like, such as "I love you like Jesus loves you."**

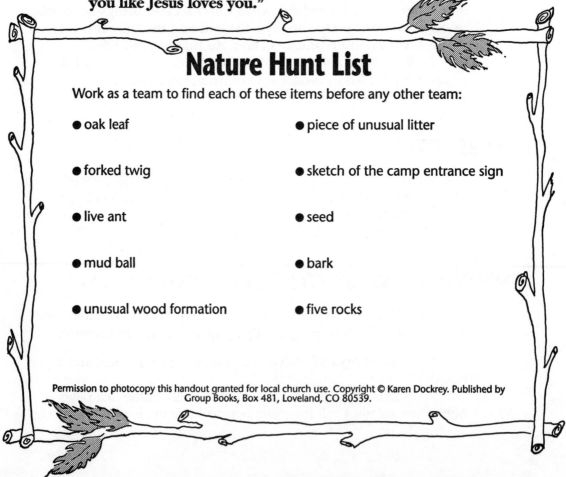

Nature Hunt List

Work as a team to find each of these items before any other team:

● oak leaf

● piece of unusual litter

● forked twig

● sketch of the camp entrance sign

● live ant

● seed

● mud ball

● bark

● unusual wood formation

● five rocks

Have kids continue to pass the books around until every person has signed every book. Each book should be in the hands of its original owner.

Say: **Count the signatures on your book. These people care about you. Even when you're in a brand new place and don't know anyone, you still have God's love and can still like yourself.**

Thanks for Me God—Have junior highers hold hands for a closing prayer. Ask each to add one sentence thanking God specifically for a way God has loved him or her. Go around the circle so kids each know when their turn is. Tell kids they can offer additional sentence prayers in random order after everyone in the circle has prayed.

THEME SNACK

Serve hot dogs with all the trimmings. Say: **Sometimes we're like hot dogs. We try to fit the bun but never quite feel like we make it. This makes us sad and frustrated.**

As kids eat, invite them to share other ways they're like hot dogs and how it makes them feel. Say: **There's one neat thing about hot dogs. We all fix them just how we want them and they all taste delicious.**

Positively point out different hot dog styles in the room. Explain how each young person has unique personality "trimmings" and is worthy of love.

GAMES

Play "Killer" (see page 24). At some point during the game, say: **In this game, killing is fun. But in life, we can kill others by the words we say.**

Ask:
● **How do we kill others with words?**
● **Why do we do it?**

Say: **Killing with words is no laughing matter. Too often we kill each other with words rather than give each other life. Use your words to give life to others rather than take it away.**

Me Booklet
I can love me because other people love me.

Signatures of people who love me:

4

Me Booklet
I can love me because God loves me.

Read Psalm 139:13-14, 23-24; Genesis 1:26-27, 31; and Ephesians 2:10. These verses are about you. Write your name in the blanks for Psalm 139:14a: "_____ praises you (God) because _____ is fearfully and wonderfully made."

Now choose another one of the passages and write your name in every place there is an I, we, us, man, him or them:

Now believe what you wrote!

1

Me Booklet
I can love me because I see the good God has created in me.

List at least 10 things you can do well. Include school skills, friend-making skills, sports skills and church skills.

1.
2.
3.
4.
5.
6.
7.
8.
9.
10.
11.

2

Me Booklet
I can show I love me by showing love for other people.

List at least 10 ways you can show love for people (Matthew 22:39).

Someone my age:

1.
2.
3.
4.
5.
6.

Someone younger than me:

7.
8.

Someone older than me:

9.
10.

3

CABIN DEVOTIONS: OVERCOMING THE BARRIERS

Have kids crawl in their bunks with their "Me Booklets." Have cabin leaders instruct kids each to share one thing they discovered from the booklet. Read aloud Matthew 22:39 and Ephesians 2:10.

Ask:

● **What's one obstacle to liking yourself you'd like to overcome this weekend?**

Pray, asking God to help kids overcome their obstacles.

SUNDAY

SEALED ORDERS

Send kids each outside with their Bible, pencil and an envelope containing their "Sealed Orders." After about 10 minutes, have kids come together and share what they wrote or drew.

CLOSING WORSHIP

Give kids each a Bible. Guide kids to find the two greatest commandments—in Matthew 22:35-40. Ask:

● **Which commandment is easiest to live? hardest?**

● **How does loving God help you love yourself?**

● **How does loving yourself help you love others?**

Give junior highers each five "warm fuzzies" and direct them to give away their fuzzies one at a time along with a compliment or a hug. Say: **Try to give away all your fuzzies before anyone else. You have to accept every fuzzy that's given to you, but you must give those fuzzies away too. As soon as you've given away all your fuzzies, shout "Fuzzie!"**

After several minutes, call time. Ask:

● **How easy was it to give your fuzzies away?**

● **What made it hard to give fuzzies?**

● **Did anyone hoard fuzzies? Why? What was the result?**

Say: **The more you concentrate on giving, the more you'll receive.**

Have junior highers each keep at least one fuzzy to remind them to give their love generously.

Hand out the affirmation sheets from the 99-Second-Love activity in Session 2. Close with prayer.

Friendship Gardens

A healthy garden requires daily care. Fruits and vegetables must be planted and nurtured. Weeds must be pulled when they're young to keep them from damaging the healthy plants. Watering must be timed and measured to ensure that the right amount of moisture reaches the roots at the proper interval.

Friendships need the same daily care. Trust and genuineness must be planted and nurtured. Weeds of frustration and fear must be uprooted early to keep them from damaging the friendship. Conversation must be measured and timed to meet the need of the moment.

This retreat encourages junior highers to see their friendships as gardens and to invest themselves in growing healthy ones.

OBJECTIVES

During this retreat junior highers will:
- experience how talking begins and enhances friendships;
- memorize Psalm 119:63 and name ways to live it;
- discuss ways to break down friendship barriers;
- list ways to build friendships;
- affirm each other with friendship-building statements;
- identify and exterminate friendship bugs; and
- give examples of friendship fruits.

SUPPLY CHECKLIST

You'll need:
- ❏ background music
- ❏ stereo
- ❏ 3×5 cards
- ❏ tape
- ❏ newsprint
- ❏ ice cream (optional)
- ❏ chocolate chips (optional)
- ❏ "Food Crisis Scavenger Hunt" handouts (page 65)
- ❏ "Worship Crisis Scavenger Hunt" handouts (page 66)
- ❏ jar of water
- ❏ masking tape
- ❏ green posterboard
- ❏ scissors
- ❏ clear glass bowl of water
- ❏ ball of yarn

For each person you'll need:
- ❏ Bible
- ❏ wooden block or brick
- ❏ permanent marker
- ❏ paper cup full of vermiculite or potting soil
- ❏ seed
- ❏ brownie
- ❏ pencil
- ❏ envelope
- ❏ blank bookmark
- ❏ paper
- ❏ tin can
- ❏ "Friendship Bug" handout (page 68)
- ❏ live leaf
- ❏ 3×5 card

For every two people you'll need:
- ❏ "Share Deck" (page 71)

RETREAT PREPARATION

● **Friends With Friends of God**—Write each word of Psalm 119:63 on a separate 3×5 card and scramble the order.

● **Brownie Break**—Prepare brownies. If you can, provide ice cream and chocolate chips to make brownie sundaes.

● **Saturday's Sealed Orders**—Read Daniel 1 and pick out truths you most want your kids to grasp. Write these truths straight from scripture with random words left out. Write all the verses on one page, photocopy one for each person and seal copies in separate envelopes.

● **Mark My Word**—Create a blank bookmark for each person by cutting paper into 1-inch strips.

● **When the Going Gets Rough**—Set up the two scavenger hunts by photocopying both sets of clues, cutting them apart and placing them each in the location indicated on the clues.

● **Friendship Bugs**—Cut out a super-size leaf from the green posterboard.

● **Enjoy the Fruit**—Fold pieces of paper in half. Write a question's number on the outside and the question on the inside of each. Kids must "flip them open" to answer the questions.

Here are the numbered questions:

1. Who's speaking?
2. How do we show we love Jesus?
3. How does verse 12 apply to friendship?
4. Give two examples of how you love your friends.
5. What is the greatest way to love according to verse 13?
6. What does Jesus call us? Why?
7. What is Jesus' command? On a scale of 1 to 10 (10=best) how well do you obey this command?

Tape the questions to one wall.

● **Sharing With Friends**—Photocopy and cut apart the "Share Deck" on page 71 so that every pair has a complete deck.

ON THE ROAD

Challenge kids to tell alphabetical stories with each word beginning with the next letter of the alphabet. At least five of the words in the sentence must be alphabetical, but they can start at any point in the alphabet. To add interest, you might let people each tell a story about themselves. For example, "I *a*te *b*anana *c*andy *d*aring *e*very *f*riend to *g*orge on something better" or "I *l*ike *m*en *n*ot *o*nly *p*leasing in looks but in personality."

THE RETREAT

FRIDAY

SESSION 1: PLANT YOUR FRIENDSHIP GARDEN

Moving Circles—Arrange equal numbers of chairs into two circles, one inside the other. Face the chairs in the inner circle outward and the chairs in the outer circle inward. As junior highers enter, direct them to sit in one of the circles.

Say: **Tell the person seated across from you about a topic I'll introduce. Then listen to that person tell you about it. I'll tell which circle goes first when I name the topic.**

RETREAT SCHEDULE

FRIDAY

8 p.m.	Session 1: Plant Your Friendship Garden
9:30 p.m.	Welcome and Rule Reminders
10 p.m.	Trust Games
11 p.m.	Brownie Break
11:30 p.m.	Cabin Devotions: Friendship Planting

SATURDAY

8 a.m.	Breakfast
8:30 a.m.	Sealed Orders
9 a.m.	Session 2: Friendship Fertilizing
10:15 a.m.	Friend Symbols
11:15 a.m.	Symbol Reports
Noon	Lunch
1 p.m.	Session 3: Bug Treatments and Weed Whacking
3 p.m.	Free Time
5 p.m.	Clean Up for Supper
6 p.m.	Supper
7 p.m.	Session 4: Harvesting the Fruits
8:30 p.m.	Sharing With Friends
10 p.m.	Cabin Devotions: Friends Forever

SUNDAY

8 a.m.	Breakfast
8:30 a.m.	Closing Worship
9:30 a.m.	Hit the Road!

Between topics, have kids each find a new partner by playing music and having kids in each circle walk in opposite directions and sit when the music stops.

Use these topics:

● time of day I do homework;
● what I like to read;
● what I want to accomplish someday;
● a person I really admire;
● my favorite food;
● something I like that others don't like;
● my favorite sport;
● what I like best about church; and
● what I like best about retreats.

Say: **The first step to beginning and keeping friendships is talking. We've practiced this with these sample topics.**

Ask:

● **What else do you talk to new friends about? to people you already know?**

Friends With Friends of God—Introduce the theme verse for the weekend by displaying it in scrambled order, one word to a card: "I am a friend to all who fear you, to all who follow your precepts" (Psalm 119:63).

Challenge kids to put the verse in order using their Bibles, but without talking. If you have a large group, make several sets of the verse cards and challenge teams to finish before the others.

After kids succeed, have them repeat the verse in unison. Remove one word after each repetition until the group recites it by memory. Congratulate their memory skills.

Ask:

● **How does being a Christian make friendship more likely?**
● **Is the way people live as important as what they say they believe? Why or why not?**

Suggest that talking is one way to start friendships.

Ask:

● **What other actions plant seeds of friendship?**

Have kids each share one obstacle that keeps them from planting friendship seeds. Write each obstacle on a brick or wooden block. As each one is named, have kids build the bricks or blocks into a wall.

After the discussion, give kids each a brick or wooden block from the wall and a marker. Have them each write how to overcome the obstacle on their brick.

When everyone is finished, have kids each read their obstacle and advice. Warmly congratulate each. Have kids use the "advised" bricks to build a bridge instead of a wall.

I'm a Friendship Planter—Ask:

● **Is it easier to let someone else start a friendship with you or to do it yourself? Why?**

After several share, gather everyone in a circle and whisper this "telephone message" to one person in the circle: **"You are a friendship planter. People want to know you."**

Have kids each whisper the message to the person on their right. Each person can whisper it only once. Ask for the message when it gets to the end. Tell kids your original message. Say: **This truth gets jumbled in real life too. Many of us doubt that anyone wants to be around us. But God created you and God doesn't make mistakes. He wants to bring out the unique and special you in your friendships.**

I'll Plant Friendships—Ask:

● **How could you begin or build a friendship during this retreat?**

Have kids each answer beginning with "I will build a friendship by ..." As kids share, give each a paper cup full of vermiculite (sprouting formula) or potting soil, and a quick sprouting seed such as an alfalfa sprout, bean or pumpkin seed. Instruct kids each to plant their seed as a symbol of friendship. Have kids each write their name on their cup. Tell them they're responsible for nurturing their seed during the weekend and after going home.

Close with prayer, asking God to help kids build healthy friendships.

RULE REMINDERS AND HOUSEKEEPING

Tape a sheet of newsprint to one wall.

Ask:

● **What builds a good friendship?**

List kids' responses on newsprint and use them to explain the reason for your rules. For example, Rule #1: "Attendance at All Sessions" gives kids more time together and more time to make friends. Rule #2: "Everyone listens to and tries to understand every comment" keeps kids from hurting each other with words and helps everyone feel accepted in the group.

TRUST GAMES

Play games that encourage trust between people. For example, do a Trust Walk: one "seeing" group member leads someone with eyes closed on a walk outside. The closed-eye person must trust the seeing partner enough to keep his or her eyes closed. See *Group Growers* (Group Books) for more community-building games.

After the games, ask:

- **How easy was it to trust?**
- **How did your partner earn your trust? betray it?**
- **How many of you opened your eyes? Why?**
- **How important is trust to friendship?**
- **What actions and attitudes build trust?**

BROWNIE BREAK

Call on a few kids to serve brownies to the others. If freezer facilities are available, bring along ice cream and chocolate chips to make brownie sundaes.

As kids eat their treats, mention that service is part of friendship. Then ask:

- **What things do you like to do for your friends?**
- **What do you like your friends to do for you?**
- **When does service get out of hand?**
- **What is the difference between serving and being used?**

Have kids each share one way they'll serve others at this retreat.

CABIN DEVOTIONS: FRIENDSHIP PLANTING

After kids are in their bunks, invite them to tell stories of how they began and grew a friendship with someone. Especially if the friend is present, encourage stories that'll help the friend feel good about being befriended. Tell the story of David and Jonathan's friendship and how they endured its trials (1 Samuel 16—21).

Ask:

- **How did David and Jonathan plant seeds? nurture them?**
- **How are our friendships similar to David and Jonathan's? different?**

SATURDAY

SEALED ORDERS

Send junior highers each to a private place with a Bible, pencil and an envelope containing their "Sealed Orders." Challenge kids to fill in the missing words.

SESSION 2: FRIENDSHIP FERTILIZING

Mark My Word—As kids enter, guide them to repeat the theme verse they memorized the night before. Give them each a blank bookmark and a pencil, and direct them to write out Psalm 119:63 on it and place it in their Bible. Say: **We'll study friends who helped each other follow God's laws.**

When the Going Gets Rough—Ask:
● **How are your plants doing this morning?**

In response to frustration that not much is happening yet, say: **Just as it takes time to grow a plant, it takes time to get to know and understand a friend. Gradually building the strength of friendships gives you power to handle the hard times. A fellow named Daniel and his three friends faced two opportunities to affirm or deny their faith and their friendships, one of which was life-threatening.**

Form two teams. Send one team on the Food Crisis Scavenger Hunt and the other team on the Worship Crisis Scavenger Hunt. Say: **I've placed clues around this room. Follow them to discover how Daniel and his friends handled their crises together.**

Give each team its first clue. Instruct kids each to take their Bible, paper and a pencil with them. Emphasize that because there are two scavenger hunts, kids need to make sure they find clues that match their hunt.

When everyone is finished, review their answers to the Food Crisis Scavenger Hunt. Use the Bible passages to discuss areas where answers differ.

Ask:
● **Why didn't Daniel want to eat the king's food?**
● **How did he get the courage to speak up?**
● **Why did his friends eat different food also?**

Say: **Friends can help each other through rough times and give each other courage to do what's right. That's positive peer pressure.**

Ask:
● **When has a friend given you courage to do what's right?**

Next, review kids' answers to the Worship Scavenger Hunt.

Ask:
● **How did the friends' experience concerning the king's food affect their actions in this situation?**

Building Friendships—Display a jar of water.

Say: **Just like we water plants to help them grow, we also "water" our friendships to make them strong.**

Food Crisis Scavenger Hunt

Cut apart each of the following clues, and hide clues #2 through #7 in appropriate places in your meeting room or outside. Leave the first clue where teams can see it.

--------------------------------✀--------------------------------

Food Clue #1—Daniel 1:3-4 describes Daniel and his friends. Circle the fact in each pair which describes them:

young	old
Babylonians	Israelites
royal	common
lowly	noble
had a favorite subject	could learn anything
quick to understand	slow to understand
ugly	handsome

Look for your next clue under the window.

--------------------------------✀--------------------------------

Food Clue #2—According to Daniel 1:4-5 why did Ashpenaz bring the boys into the court? There are three reasons.

Look for your next clue on the ceiling.

--------------------------------✀--------------------------------

Food Clue #3—What new names did Daniel and his friends receive? See Daniel 1:6-7.

Look for your next clue under the stairs.

--------------------------------✀--------------------------------

Food Clue #4—What problem did Daniel and his friends face? See Daniel 1:5-10.

Look for your next clue by the fireplace.

--------------------------------✀--------------------------------

Food Clue #5—What steps did Daniel take to do what was right? See Daniel 1:8-12.

Look for your next clue on a leader's back.

--------------------------------✀--------------------------------

Food Clue #6—What was the result of Daniel's test? See Daniel 1:15-16.

Look for your next clue under a table.

--------------------------------✀--------------------------------

Food Clue #7—What three gifts did God give Daniel and his friends? See Daniel 1:17, 20. How would you use these gifts?

Congratulations! Take a seat in a chair.

--------------------------------✀--------------------------------

Worship Crisis Scavenger Hunt

Cut apart the following clues and hide clues #2 through #8 in appropriate places in your meeting room or outside. Leave the first clue where teams can see it.

- ✀ -

Worship Clue #1—What were Daniel's friends commanded to worship? See Daniel 3:1, 5.

Look for your next clue under the window.

- ✀ -

Worship Clue #2—According to Daniel 3:6 what would happen to anyone who refused to worship that image?

Look for your next clue on the ceiling.

- ✀ -

Worship Clue #3—Who told on Daniel's friends? See Daniel 1:12.

Look for your next clue under the stairs.

- ✀ -

Worship Clue #4—How did King Nebuchadnezzar feel about the friends refusing to worship? See Daniel 3:13-15.

Look for your next clue by the fireplace.

- ✀ -

Worship Clue #5—Why did Shadrach, Meshach and Abednego not defend themselves before the king? See Daniel 3:16-18. Do you think God would do for you what he did for Shadrach, Meshach and Abednego? Why or why not?

Look for your next clue on a leader's back.

- ✀ -

Worship Clue #6—How did King Nebuchadnezzar respond to the friends' testimony about God? See Daniel 3:19-23.

Look for your next clue by the clock.

- ✀ -

Worship Clue #7—Who do you think the fourth person was? What does this situation tell you about God's faithfulness during "hot" times? See Daniel 3:22-25.

Look for your next clue under a table.

- ✀ -

Worship Clue #8—How did King Nebuchadnezzar respond to the friends not being burned? See Daniel 3:24-30.

Congratulations! Take a seat in a chair.

- ✀ -

Ask:

● **In what ways do you water your friendships to help them grow?**

● **How does watering a friendship prepare it for a crisis, such as a fight?**

As kids share ideas, direct them each to add a bit of water to the plants they planted during Session 1.

After everyone has shared, lead the group to affirm each junior higher one at a time by saying this in unison: "You, (name of junior higher), are a friendship-builder."

Friendship-Building—Have junior highers each write their name on the outside of a tin can using a permanent marker. Have them attach their cans to the wall with masking tape. Say: **This weekend, fill each can with friendship-building statements and actions. For example, you might give encouragement by writing the way you see a friend stand up for Jesus this weekend. Put at least one friendship-builder in every person's can.**

Keep paper for notes near the cans. Make sure you and your adult leaders add a note to each can.

FRIEND SYMBOLS

Allow kids about an hour of free time. Give this assignment: **During your free time, find something that symbolizes or demonstrates friendship. You may not destroy anything to bring it back. If you cannot bring it, we'll go with you to see it or have you describe it.**

Allow kids to work together, but insist that each bring something different. After an hour, call kids together and have them each explain their symbol. Warmly praise each young person.

SESSION 3: BUG TREATMENTS AND WEED WHACKING

Friendship Bugs—As kids enter, say: **Sometimes pests get into our friendships. How can we get rid of the bugs without killing the friendship?**

Give kids each a "Friendship Bug" handout to complete.

Hold up a super-size paper leaf as junior highers tell about their bugs. Tear off a small section as each bug is shared.

Ask:

● **Why do these little bugs have such power to destroy friendship?**

Friendship Bug

Draw or describe a bug that eats away at friendship. A friendship bug feeds on friendship in a destructive way, sometimes working unnoticed until the damage has been done. This can be a general problem like "jealousy" or a specific problem like "my friend gets jealous whenever I talk to anyone else."

● **How can we recognize them before they do damage?**
● **How can we repair damage once they attack?**

Exterminate the Bugs—Collect the bugs and shuffle them. Give each bug to someone besides its creator. Form pairs. Say: **Work with your partner to write a TV or radio commercial for an insecticide that would keep your bugs from attacking your friendship or would get rid of it once it comes. Choose friendship actions from Romans 12:9-21 to help you get started.**

When teams are ready, have them each perform their commercial. Affirm each pair.

When I Bug Friendships—Say: **Sometimes we create our own friendship bugs. We do things we can't believe we did. We say things we don't mean. We get shy about saying what we want to say. We have trouble loving like we want to.**

Give junior highers each a section from the leaf. Have them each write on it something they do that eats away at friendships.

Say: **Let's take our bug-infested leaf sections outside where they belong and release them where they can do no more harm.**

Guide kids to tear their leaf sections, burn them or otherwise dispose of them so they can no longer be read or discovered.

Turn Over a New Leaf—While still outside, focus on group friendships by asking:

● **What bugs threaten our group's unity and happiness?**

● **What do we do to tear our group down rather than build it up?**

● **Why do we need each other's friendship?**

Give kids each a live leaf and have them write on it actions that could promote friendship in the group. Collect the leaves and display them in the meeting room in a clear glass bowl filled with water.

SESSION 4: HARVESTING THE FRUITS

Enjoy the Fruit—As junior highers enter, give each a pencil. Have kids each walk around the room and write an answer based on John 15:9-17 to each of the seven questions you taped to the wall.

After everyone is finished, take the questions from the wall, hand them out and have kids read aloud each question and its answers.

Fruits of Friendship—Ask:

● **What do you think the fruits are in verse 16?**

Suggest that the verse 16 fruits might be the fruit of the Spirit listed in Galatians 5:22-23. Say: **Choose one of the fruits from Galatians 5:22-23 and tell how it enhances friendship.**

Encourage several examples for each fruit.

God and I Are Friends—Point out that every teenager in the room is capable of loving like Jesus once he or she becomes a Christian. Give kids each a Bible and have them look up John 15:12-16. Say: **One at a time, read aloud John 15:12-16 with your name inserted for every "you," "he" and "his," and Jesus' name inserted for every "I" and "me."**

For example, if Sarah read the passage, she would say: "Jesus' command is this: Love each other as Jesus has loved Sarah. Greater love has no one than this, that Sarah lay down Sarah's life for Sarah's friends ... Instead, Jesus has called Sarah friend, for everything Jesus learned from his Father he made known to Sarah. Sarah did not choose Jesus but Jesus chose Sarah and appointed Sarah to go and bear fruit—fruit that will last."

If your group is large, have kids read the passages to each other in small groups.

A Web of Friendship—Say: **Now let's demonstrate our love for each other with a fun activity.**

Have kids form a circle. Hold up a ball of yarn and say: **I'll**

throw this ball of yarn to someone who's been a friend to me during this retreat and tell how he or she has been a friend. That person will then throw the yarn to someone who's been a friend and tell how. We'll continue throwing until we're all connected by a web of friendship.

Monitor the process and watch for junior highers who may not be getting the ball as often as others. Toss to them when your turns come.

Ask:

● **How is this ball like friendship? like group closeness?**

Pass a pair of scissors and instruct kids to cut a piece of yarn to keep as a reminder of their unity with the group.

SHARING WITH FRIENDS

After a brief stretch break, have kids arrange the chairs in twosomes all over the room. Direct kids each to sit in one of the chairs across from the person of their choice. Encourage adult leaders to participate in this activity. Place a "Share Deck" on the floor between each twosome.

Say: **Between you is a deck of cards. On "go," turn the top card over and complete the statement. Talk as long as you want on that topic and then put it at the bottom of the stack and draw another.**

After five minutes, have kids find new partners. Say: **Repeat the sharing process with your new partner, starting with the deck where it is.**

After another five minutes, call everyone together and ask:

● **How is this like making friends?**

● **What new things did you learn about one of your partners?**

● **What did you enjoy about this experience?**

CABIN DEVOTIONS: FRIENDS FOREVER

As kids settle into their beds, invite them each to share a problem they have with friends and then how they think God wants them to solve it. Don't allow anyone to share a problem without a possible solution. After each person shares, invite others to add ideas. Discourage kids from using names. Encourage kids to read Romans 12:9-21 and Proverbs 17:17 for solution ideas.

Share Deck

Photocopy and cut apart these cards so that every two people have a full deck of cards.

My favorite sandwich is . . .	My favorite TV show is . . .
After school I like to . . .	Before school I like to . . .
A book I really like is . . .	I like to listen to . . .
It really bugs me when . . .	I love it when . . .
I'm scared of . . .	I like a friend to . . .
I wish I could . . .	I make friends by . . .
The quality I most like about God is . . .	

SUNDAY

CLOSING WORSHIP

Instruct kids to bring their plants to the closing worship. When everyone has arrived, ask:

● **How has the seed changed since you planted it?**

Some plants have likely sprouted by now, while others are planted so deeply they aren't visible yet.

Ask:

● **How do these changes parallel friendship?**
● **What dangers did your plant encounter?**
● **How do these dangers parallel friendship?**

Give kids each a permanent marker. Have kids each write a friendship verse such as Proverbs 17:17 on their plant's cup. Say: **Every time you see the plant, compare it to your friendships and think about how you're nurturing them.**

Challenge kids to recite Psalm 119:63 from memory. Say: **Just as you plan to take steps toward closeness in your personal friendships, take steps to make this group a closer, more friendly one.**

Give kids each a 3×5 card and a pencil. Have them each write their name on their card. Collect the cards, shuffle them and redistribute them to the group.

Take the group outside and say: **Find an organic item such as a leaf or a flower that represents something you admire about the person named on your card. For example, if your person is an encourager, you might find a branch to show how the person "supports" others in the group.**

Be sure to instruct kids not to damage any living plants in getting their items.

After about five minutes, call everyone together and have kids each share their item with the group.

Say: **We all bring special qualities to the group that together make up a unified, living organism—the church.**

Close with prayer, asking God to equip kids to grow a close group.

"Why Can't My Parents Understand Me?"

Many family problems stem from differences in perspective. The parent whose presence determines the success of his or her office meeting may not understand a junior higher who frequently asks for time off from work. And a junior higher who knows anyone can flip burgers doesn't understand why a parent can't skip work to do something with him or her.

This retreat, based on 1 John, guides junior highers and their parents to overcome blind points—family problems parents or kids can't see—and focus on building unity. Junior highers and parents meet jointly at church for the first session and then junior highers continue their study at a retreat site.

Explain to your kids that "parent" means the adult they each live with. It can be a biological parent, adoptive parent, stepparent, foster parent, grandparent or a guardian. Show sensitivity by using "parent" more often than "parents" and by including questions about the parent who may not live with the junior higher.

OBJECTIVES

During this retreat junior highers will:
- discover that other junior highers also struggle with family issues;
- talk with one or both of their parents;
- name at least one way they're like their parents;
- notice the ways perspective affects understanding; and
- create a covenant of concrete actions to promote understanding at home.

SUPPLY CHECKLIST

You'll need:
- ❑ 3×5 cards
- ❑ paper
- ❑ masking tape
- ❑ sandwiches
- ❑ soft drinks
- ❑ newsprint
- ❑ Chex party mix or Reese's Peanut Butter Cups

For each person you'll need:
- ❑ "Name-O-Rama" handout (page 77)
- ❑ pencil
- ❑ marker
- ❑ Bible
- ❑ "Sealed Orders" handout (page 80)
- ❑ envelope
- ❑ white blindfold
- ❑ scissors
- ❑ piece of clay
- ❑ pipe cleaner
- ❑ "Family Covenant Offering" handout (page 83)
- ❑ "Wish List" handout (page 85)
- ❑ 2-foot long piece of string

RETREAT PREPARATION

● **Newly-Teenager Game**—Find two to five parent-teenager pairs to play the Newly-Teenager Game. Enlist at least two leaders to lead small groups. Set up four to 10 game chairs in a row at the front of the room.

● **Late Night Share Time and Snack**—Bring sandwiches and soft drinks for everyone.

● **Sealed Orders**—Make one copy of the "Sealed Orders" handout for each person. Insert copies in separate envelopes.

● **Blindfold Obstacle Course**—Use available items such as tables and chairs to create a series of obstacles in the main meeting room. Designate a door, window or sign as the ending point.

● **The Way We See Each Other**—Use newsprint and a marker to create four life-size full-body outlines. Make one outline of a 2-year-old, one of a 5-year-old, one of a 10-year-old and one of a junior higher. Write the age each outline represents at the top of each sheet of newsprint.

● **Family Snacks**—Bring along Chex party mix or Reese's Peanut Butter Cups.

RETREAT SCHEDULE

FRIDAY

7:30 p.m.	Session 1: More Than a Game
9:30 p.m.	Depart for Retreat Site
11 p.m.	Welcome and Rule Reminders
11:15 p.m.	Late Night Share Time and Snack

SATURDAY

8 a.m.	Breakfast
8:30 a.m.	Sealed Orders
9 a.m.	Session 2: Turn On the Light
10:30 a.m.	Blindfold Games
12:30 p.m.	Lunch
1:30 p.m.	Session 3: A Matter of Perspective
3 p.m.	My Tip For Family Happiness
5:30 p.m.	Clean Up for Supper
6 p.m.	Supper
7 p.m.	Session 4: Covenant Offering
8:30 p.m.	Tip Presentations
9:30 p.m.	Family Snacks
10 p.m.	Cabin Devotions

SUNDAY

8 a.m.	Breakfast
8:30 a.m.	Closing Worship
9 a.m.	Pack Up, Pick Up, Clean Up
Noon	Arrive Home!

ON THE ROAD

Form two teams. Have teams each create a song about each person in the other group. Encourage teams to use popular tunes and to make the songs edifying.

THE RETREAT

FRIDAY

SESSION 1: MORE THAN A GAME

Game Time—This first retreat session includes parents of junior highers. As parents and junior highers arrive, give them each a "Name-O-Rama" handout and a pencil. Have parents and junior highers each obtain a signature for each block.

When everyone is finished, say: **Though fun is an important part of parent-teenage relationships, it's not the only important element. Communication and understanding are also crucial elements of family living. Let's play a game that demonstrates these elements.**

Newly-Teenager Game—Enthusiastically announce the family game by saying: **You may have heard of *The Dating Game* and *The Newlywed Game*. This game takes relationships one step further. It's called The Newly-Teenager Game. It discovers how well junior highers and their parents understand each other.**

Invite the two to five parent-teenager pairs—who you contacted ahead of time—to sit in the game chairs. Have parents and teenagers each pick up five cards and a marker.

Say: **In a moment the junior highers and their parents will each go to separate rooms and answer the questions we'll later ask their partner. We'll see just how well kids and parents understand each other.**

Send the kids to one room and the parents to another—each with a leader.

At this point you have three groups with three leaders: parents, kids and audience. Have group leaders each follow these instructions that pertain to their group.

Name-O-Rama

Fill out this sheet. You can have only one name per box. Find someone who . . .

Is wearing red.	Has a sister.
Has been treated unfairly by a parent.	Likes to stay up late.
Likes to go to bed early.	Likes her mom.
Likes her dad.	Likes his mom.
Likes his dad.	Likes his son.
Likes her son.	Likes her daughter.
Likes his daughter.	Wants to be in junior high again.
Has homework to do this weekend.	Brought a Bible to the retreat.
Brought a mom to this session.	Is over 18.
Brought a dad to this session.	Is under 18.

● **Parents**—Have the leader instruct the parents to privately write on separate cards a completion of each of these statements:

1. I most worry about ...
2. I show my teenager I love him/her by ...
3. I get most frustrated with my teenager when ...
4. I want my teenager to understand ...
5. I'm proud of my teenager because ...

Have the leader instruct the parents each to number the back of each card and keep the cards in order face down.

● **Kids**—Have the leader instruct the kids to privately write on separate cards a completion of each of these statements:

1. I am happiest when ...
2. I think my parent doesn't understand when ...
3. I trust my parent when ...
4. I most want my parent to know that I ...
5. I really need my parent to ...

Have the leader instruct the kids each to number the back of each card and keep the cards in order face down.

● **Audience**—Form teams of two or three, mixing parents and kids evenly. Give teams each paper and a marker. Say: **Let's see which team can make the longest list of communication barriers. Later we'll discover communication-clearers that can break down these barriers.**

Motivate teams by continually reporting which team is ahead. Call time when the leaders cue you that the parent-teenager pairs have finished. Instruct the teams each to roll up their list and let no one see it until the right time is announced.

Cue the leaders to bring in the kids and parents. Have parent-teenager partners sit together with their answer cards face down in their laps. Read the open-ended statements again—kids' statements first, then parents'. This time have partners each answer the way they think their partner answered. After each answer, cue the partner to lift the card that gives the answer. Award points for matched answers.

Say: **Parents and teenagers sometimes struggle to understand each other. Loving like Jesus loves can make understanding and care a reality. Tonight and during the weekend we'll be studying passages from a book that focuses on Jesus' love: 1 John.**

Communication-Clearers—Have the audience teams each tape to the wall their list of communication barriers. Applaud the team with the longest list. If you had no audience because of a small group, list barriers now.

Assign teams each a list other than the one they wrote. Say: **Find communication-clearers that'll overcome the barriers on your assigned list. These clearers are ways parents and teenag-**

ers can listen to each other, understand each other and encourage each other to live the Christian life. Refer to 1 John 3:11-18 and 4:18-21 for ideas. You have about five minutes.

When everyone's finished, have teams report.

We're a Team—Call everyone together. Give people each a 3×5 card. Say: **Write a recipe for clearer communication in your relationship with your parent or teenager. Use 1 John 3:11-18 and 4:18-21 with the communication-clearers we've just discussed. After you write your recipe reread it to be sure it's constructive—not destructive.**

When everyone's finished, have kids each exchange their recipe card with their parent's. Have parents and kids each pray for God's guidance as they follow the recipes.

Say: **You've demonstrated that loving a family is more than a game. It takes daily work and commitment. We teenagers and sponsors will spend the weekend learning better how to love our families. We encourage parents to the same while at home.**

Close with a group hug and choruses such as "Blest Be the Tie That Binds" and "We Are One in the Spirit."

After the closing, have kids pack up and leave for the retreat site.

LATE NIGHT SHARE TIME AND SNACK

Serve sandwiches and soft drinks. Form groups of 15 or fewer. Then gather groups each in a circle. Have kids introduce themselves within their groups by completing the following statement, each using the first letter of their name to start their response to the statement:

● I'm (first name) and my parents are _____ like me.

For example, one teenager might say, "I'm Hanna and my parents are happy like me." Before saying their part, have junior highers each repeat what all others have said. For example, if Hanna was the third teenager to respond, she might say: "This is Maria and her parents are majorly excited about church—like she is. This is Paul and his parents are particular about the way they treat their friends—like he is. I'm Hanna and my parents are happy like I am."

After everyone has responded, have volunteers read aloud Proverbs 3:12; 10:1; 15:20; and 17:6.

Ask:

● **What does it take for you to be proud of your parents?**
● **What does it take for them to be proud of you?**

Close the share time with prayer. Encourage kids each to thank God for their parents.

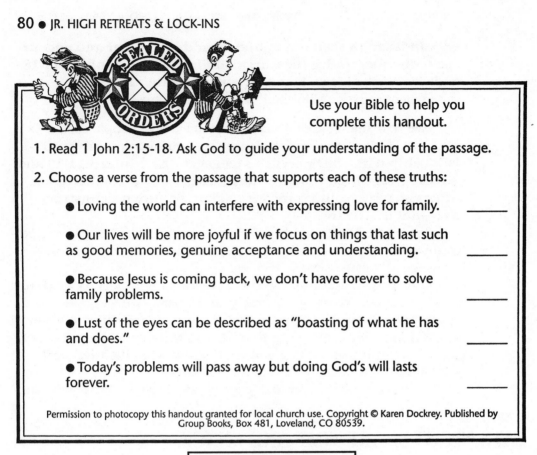

Use your Bible to help you complete this handout.

1. Read 1 John 2:15-18. Ask God to guide your understanding of the passage.

2. Choose a verse from the passage that supports each of these truths:

● Loving the world can interfere with expressing love for family. _____

● Our lives will be more joyful if we focus on things that last such as good memories, genuine acceptance and understanding. _____

● Because Jesus is coming back, we don't have forever to solve family problems. _____

● Lust of the eyes can be described as "boasting of what he has and does." _____

● Today's problems will pass away but doing God's will lasts forever. _____

SATURDAY

SEALED ORDERS

Have kids each go outside to a private place with their Bible, a pencil and an envelope containing their "Sealed Orders."

As kids return, have them share their discoveries.

SESSION 2: TURN ON THE LIGHT

Blindfold Obstacle Course—Before kids enter, blindfold them with white blindfolds. Challenge them to make it through the obstacle course you've set up in the room. Tell kids the goal is to get to a designated point on the other side of the room.

Once kids make it across, ask:

● **How did this experience make you feel?**

● **Did any of you try to see around the blindfold? Why or why not?**

Explain that most of us have times in our families when we act like we have blindfolds on. We can't always tell where we're going or why we're going there. Removing the blindfolds would bring deeper happiness at home.

Give junior highers each a marker and say: **Write on your blindfold at least 10 areas of "blindness" between kids and their parents. These can be areas you struggle with in your home or areas someone you know struggles with.**

Identify the Blinders—Gather kids in a circle and have them blindfold themselves. While they're blindfolded, ask:
● **What areas of blindness did you write on your blindfold?**
● **What problems do they cause?**
Allow kids to take off their blindfolds. Ask:
● **How is a blindfold like living in a family?**
After kids respond, have them each put their blindfold in their pocket or attach it to their clothing to use later.

Have volunteers read aloud 1 John 1:5-9. Ask:
● **What do these verses teach about blindfolds?**

Take Off Your Blinders—Have kids each get their blindfold and circle three areas of blindness they most want to remove in their family. Have kids share the areas they circled. Then ask:
● **What actions can you take to remove your blinders?**
Give kids each a pair of scissors and have them cut two eye-holes in their blindfold as blinder-removing actions are discussed.

After kids share, have them each hold up their blindfold and look through it. Ask:
● **How well can you see each other?**
Say: **The only blinders you can remove are your own. Though your actions can motivate your parents to remove their blinders, they may not. Even if they don't, removing your blinders can bring joy to you and the people you come in contact with.**
Close with prayer.

BLINDFOLD GAMES

Play games with blindfolds. Possibilities include:
● Form teams and have a relay race. Have kids each run to a chair, sit in it while tying on a blindfold, run back toward the voices on their team, circle the team and then give the blindfold to the next person in line.
● Play Drop the Handkerchief.
● Invite teams each to make up a game that uses blindfolds and have them each teach their game to the other teams.

SESSION 3: A MATTER OF PERSPECTIVE

The Way We See Each Other—Tape to the wall the four life-size full-body outlines. Say: **Go around the room and sketch or write on each outline how you think your parents saw you when you were these ages.**

When kids are finished, ask:

● **Why is it hard for parents to change their perception of you?**

● **How do our perceptions affect how well we understand each other?**

● **How can we find whether our perceptions are right or wrong?**

Say: **The more parents and kids share their perceptions, fears, hopes and ideas with each other, the better they'll understand each other. As you seek to understand your parents, talking with them becomes easier. They in turn may try to understand you better.**

I See the Son in You—Form pairs and have kids each share a family issue they want to pray about. Challenge kids to pray together for each other's specific parent issues.

I'll See It Your Way—Give kids each paper and a pencil. Say: **Write about a frustrating situation in your family and describe how you think your parents see that situation.**

Collect the papers and redistribute them to the pairs formed in the previous activity. Have kids role-play a solution for each problem. After the role plays, invite others to add ideas.

Ask:

● **How else might parents or kids see these situations?**

● **What other ideas do you have for solving these problems?**

MY TIP FOR FAMILY HAPPINESS

Say: **During free time, get together with at least one other person and prepare a skit, commercial or presentation of a tip for getting along with parents.**

SESSION 4: COVENANT OFFERING

Here's the Problem—As kids enter, give each a piece of clay and a pipe cleaner. Have them each shape something that represents a specific struggle they face with their parents. Explain that this can be an issue such as dating, a frustration such as curfews, or something else that keeps love from flowing in families.

When everyone is finished, form groups of four to six. Have kids each share their creation in their group.

There's Only So Much Time—Invite a volunteer to read aloud 1 John 2:15-18. Give kids each paper and a pencil.

Ask:

● **Because we have no guarantee of even one more hour of life, what might you do to solve the family struggle you shaped?**

After a few kids share, have kids each write what they'd do to solve the problem if they had only one hour to live.

Invite kids to share what they wrote. Say: **Because we have no guarantee of tomorrow, let's make sure each word and action builds closeness rather than tears it down.**

Covenant Offerings—Give kids each a "Family Covenant Offering" handout. Guide kids to complete the handout.

Have a few volunteers read their covenants to the group. Encourage junior highers each to take their covenant home and give them to their parent.

FAMILY COVENANT OFFERING

Before God I vow to:

understand _____;

listen to _____;

solve problems by _____;

do my part in the family by _____;

share my feelings more clearly by _____; and

_____.

Close by having junior highers each pray for the people on both sides of them.

TIP PRESENTATIONS

Call on each pair or group to present the tip it prepared during free time for getting along with parents. Encourage thunderous applause from the audience after each tip.

FAMILY SNACKS

Serve snacks that require more than one ingredient to taste good; for example, Chex party mix or Reese's Peanut Butter Cups. Say: **It takes more than one ingredient to make these snacks good. In a similar way, it takes more than just you or me to make a family. Parents and kids can create happiness together just like a handful of party mix makes my mouth happier than just a pretzel.**

CABIN DEVOTIONS

Have the cabin leader gather cabin mates together and ask:
● **What have you learned about family life during this weekend?**
● **What do you want to change in your family?**
● **How do you plan to do it?**
● **What do you now understand better about your parents?**

SUNDAY

CLOSING WORSHIP

As kids enter the worship area, give each a "Wish List" handout and a pencil. Have kids each complete the handout.
After kids complete the handout, ask:
● **What do you wish for your family?**
Read aloud 1 John 5:13-15. Encourage kids each to review their wishes and choose one they'd like to request from God.
Ask:
● **What's your request and how do you think God will answer it? Why?**

Wish List

What do you wish your family could be like? Write four qualities you'd like in your family using the letters of the word "wish." The letters can come at the beginning, middle or end of the word.

W

I

S

H

Encourage kids each to let God use them in their family—whatever that may be. Add a story from your own family of a time God worked a dramatic change, and a time the change was more gradual or mainly in you. Invite kids to share whether they think their requests will change mostly them, mostly their parents or both.

Give kids each a 3×5 card, a pencil and a 2-foot long piece of string. Have kids each write their request on their 3×5 card. Then have them each poke a hole in their card with their pencil and thread their string through the hole.

Take the group outside and have kids each tie their request to the branches of one tree. Then have kids form a circle around the tree and hold hands.

Say: **This is our family prayer tree. Just as this tree now holds our cards, so God now holds our requests near his heart. Let's thank God for taking our requests upon himself.**

Gather everyone in a circle. Lead kids in an add-on prayer. Starting with the person on your right, go around the circle and have kids each offer a sentence prayer, adding on to what the person on their left just prayed. You close.

After the closing, have someone remove the cards from the tree and throw them away.

God's Good Gift of Sex

Sex.

Junior highers whisper about it, wonder about it and giggle when it's mentioned. Why are they—and we—so uneasy about sex? Because it's incredibly important and tremendously powerful. It's a marvelous gift from God.

How can we guide junior highers to understand sex and express it according to God's plan? This retreat provides questions and activities to lead kids to discover and live in God's guidelines for this beautiful gift.

OBJECTIVES

During this retreat junior highers will:
- discover that sex expressed God's way is good;
- realize that the Bible has a great deal to say about sex;
- pinpoint twisted truths about sex;
- understand why God's guidelines for sex make sense;
- list ways to say no to sex before marriage; and
- name ways they'll be honest in relationships.

SUPPLY CHECKLIST

You'll need:
❑ newsprint
❑ bag of M&Ms
❑ overhead transparencies
❑ "Sex Jeopardy Answers"
   (page 91)
❑ overhead projector
❑ "Sex Jeopardy Questions"
   (page 92)
❑ sandwich supplies, chips
   and cookies
❑ Kenny Wood and Billy
   Crockett's *Love Waiting* album
   (Word) or something like it
❑ "Lines" (page 97)
❑ paper sack
❑ popped popcorn kernels
❑ trash bag
❑ unpopped popcorn kernels
❑ two mixing bowls
❑ two spoons or knives
❑ toothpicks
❑ popcorn flavorings
❑ fruit juice or soft drinks

For each person you'll need:
❑ construction paper
❑ pen or pencil
❑ Bible
❑ envelope
❑ "Sealed Orders" (page 94)
❑ "Media Search Instructions"
   (page 95)
❑ paper
❑ marker
❑ credit-card-size posterboard
❑ fine-tip marker

For each group of four to six you'll need:
❑ posterboard
❑ scissors
❑ masking tape
❑ assorted magazines, album
   jackets, posters and tabloids

For each team of three to four you'll need:
❑ "Sex Jeopardy Rules" (page 90)

RETREAT PREPARATION

● **Sex Jeopardy**—To play the Sex Jeopardy game, photocopy the "Sex Jeopardy Answers" onto an overhead transparency and tape slips of paper over each answer box. Project the game onto the wall.

● **Sealed Orders**—Make a copy of the "Sealed Orders" for each person, and seal each in an envelope.

● **Sex Media Search**—Set up a station for ever four to six junior highers. On each table, put posterboard, scissors, masking tape and an assortment of magazines, album jackets, posters and tabloids.

● **God Made You Lovable**—Cut a credit-card-size piece of posterboard for each person.

● **Under-Chair Questions**—Write these Bible references on strips of paper and tape one to the bottom of each chair in the meeting room: Genesis 2:23-25; Exodus 20:14; Psalm 37:4; Proverbs 5:3-6; Proverbs 5:18-19; Song of Songs; Matthew 6:33; 1 Corinthians 6:18-20;

1 Corinthians 10:13; 1 Corinthians 13:4-8; and Hebrews 13:4. It's okay if two kids have the same passage.

● **Line Crushers**—Photocopy and cut apart the statements from "Lines." Place the lines in a paper sack.

● **Popcorn Games**—Write out the word "popcorn." Then photocopy the word and cut apart the letters. Make enough copies so each person will have one letter.

ON THE ROAD

Challenge pairs or trios to write new verses to popular love songs, describing God's view of love. Use a cassette recorder to tape kids' creations. Play the new love songs as kids sing along.

THE RETREAT

FRIDAY

SESSION 1: SEX IS MORE THAN A GAME

Getting to Know You—As kids enter, form a circle. If you have more than 20 kids, form two circles. Say: **This weekend we'll be studying a great gift of God: sex. During this weekend we hope to discover ways to tell the myths from the truths.**

Write these four open-ended statements on a sheet of newsprint:
● My favorite TV show is ...
● I love to ...
● I hate to ...
● My favorite part of school is ...

Tape the newsprint to the wall. Say: **Let's practice distinguishing myths from truths. Each of you complete the statements, but lie about one. The rest of us will try to discover the lie.**

Call on volunteers to go first, but be sure everyone gets a turn. After each person responds, have the class vote on which response was a lie. Award one point to each person who guesses correctly.

After everyone completes the exercise, tally kids' scores and award the winner a bag of M&Ms.

RETREAT SCHEDULE

FRIDAY

8 p.m.	Welcome and Rule Reminders
8:15 p.m.	Session 1: Sex Is More Than a Game
9:45 p.m.	Sandwich Snack
10 p.m.	Free Time
11 p.m.	Cabin Devotions: Good Plans

SATURDAY

8 a.m.	Breakfast
8:30 a.m.	Sealed Orders
9 a.m.	Session 2: Media Messages and Myths
10:30 a.m.	Free Time
Noon	Lunch
1 p.m.	Session 3: Line Levelers
2:30 p.m.	Free Time
4:30 p.m.	Shaving Cream Fight
5 p.m.	Clean Up for Supper
6 p.m.	Supper
7 p.m.	Session 4: Love Counselor
8:30 p.m.	Popcorn Games
9:30 p.m.	Popcorn Snack
10 p.m.	Cabin Devotions: Handbook Review

SUNDAY

8 a.m.	Breakfast
8:30 a.m.	Closing Worship
9:30 a.m.	Depart

Sex Jeopardy—Say: **We're all curious and embarrassed about sex. Talking about sex is uncomfortable partly because it's so personal, but also because it's so important. And our society lies about sex. Often it's hard to know what's true.**
Ask:

● **How do you tell the lies from the truth?**

● **What's our one source of accurate information about sex?**

Say: **Because God created sex, he understands its purpose. We're here this weekend to discover ways to make our sex lives the best they can be. Since God created sex, Christians ought to have the best sex lives. Right?**

Form teams of three or four to play Sex Jeopardy. Give teams each a copy of the "Sex Jeopardy Rules" and go over the rules. Also photocopy the "Sex Jeopardy Questions" to check responses.

Sex Handbooks—Give junior highers each a piece of construction paper, and a pen or pencil. Say: **Fold your paper in half to form a booklet. Write your name in the top right corner of the front page, and title the booklet "Sex Handbook."**

Have kids each write inside the front cover at least one truth and one myth they discovered about sex during this session. Have kids keep their handbooks private, but don't discourage sharing ideas.

Sex Jeopardy Rules

Rule #1—The team who has a player with the birthday closest to today goes first. That team chooses the first category and point value. The leader uncovers the answer.

Rule #2—Anyone who thinks they know the question, stands. The first one standing gets the first try. If correct, points are awarded to that team. If not, points are deducted and the second person who stood gets to guess. Control of category and point value goes to whichever team answers correctly.

Rule #3—Team members may collaborate to decide the answer before a team member stands—but not once the team member is standing.

Rule # 4—This is an open-book game. Please use your Bible to discover Sex Jeopardy answers that have Bible references.

Sex Jeopardy Answers

POINTS	THE BIBLE	WHY WAIT?	PRESSURES	LIMITS	WHAT?
10	Adam's reaction to seeing Eve for the first time. It can be translated "Wow!" (Genesis 2:23).	Sexual immorality sins against this (1 Corinthians 6:18).	A place where sex outside of marriage is promoted almost any hour of the day.	The person in the relationship who has the most sensitive conscience.	Motivates us to do right (Romans 13:9-10).
20	The Bible phrase for sex. (Genesis 4:1).	AIDS, chlamydia and herpes.	Because God created us to long for someone to love us forever and to express that love through sex.	When sexual limits should be defined.	The amount of time a marriage built on romantic love typically lasts.
30	The content of Song of Songs.	A situation with no good options: either raising the baby alone, letting parents raise the baby or giving the baby up for adoption.	Decide whether you'd be proud if someone else knew what you're doing sexually.	Stay above the neck, stay below the knee.	A good and responsible choice following an unplanned pregnancy that gives a child to a couple who could otherwise never have one.
40	Described in Proverbs 5:18-19 and 1 Corinthians 7:2-5.	God knows more than us, loves us more than we can ever comprehend and wants to provide for us the very best.	We have many years between puberty and marriage but Bible kids got married young to someone of their parents' choosing.	How long and how far.	Talk, spend time with friends, complete a project together, take care of someone else or play sports.
50	Promise about sex in 1 Corinthians 10:13.	Usually an untrue statement designed to use you rather than love you. An example is: "If you love me, you'll let me."	David and Bathsheba; Abraham and Hagar (2 Samuel 11:4; Genesis 16:3-4).	When your spouse is out of town, when one of you is sick or when you abstain for a time to seek the Lord.	When your desire for sex and love begins.

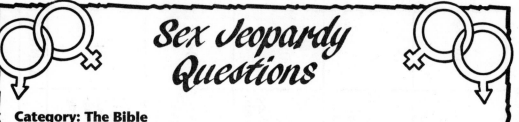

Sex Jeopardy Questions

Category: The Bible
10—What is "this is now bone of my bones and flesh of my flesh"?
20—What is "lay with"?
30—What is a description of Solomon's wife?
40—What is married people enjoying sex?
50—What is we have the power to wait for sex until marriage?

Category: Why Wait?
10—What is our own body?
20—What are incurable sexually transmitted diseases?
30—What is pregnancy outside of marriage?
40—What are the reasons we should obey God's command to wait until marriage to have sex?
50—What is a "come on" or "line"?

Category: Pressures
10—What is television?
20—What is the reason we know sex is good?
30—What is one way to help you wait for sex until marriage?
40—What are the differences in pressure felt by Bible kids and kids today?
50—Who are Bible couples who had sex outside of marriage?

Category: Limits
10—Who is the person who should set the limits in a relationship?
20—What is before a tempting situation arises?
30—What are two good limits for unmarried couples?
40—What are two types of limits?
50—What are three times you'll need sexual control after marriage?

Category: What?
10—What is love?
20—What is six to 12 months?
30—What is adoption?
40—What are things to do on a date that don't involve sex?
50—What is puberty?

As kids finish, have them each decorate the front cover of their sex handbook. Gather the handbooks for use during a later session. Assure junior highers you'll let no one read their handbooks.

SANDWICH SNACK

Display cold cuts, condiments, bread, chips and cookies. Encourage junior highers each to make a sandwich as you play contemporary Christian music. An excellent album encouraging God's view of sex is Kenny Wood and Billy Crockett's *Love Waiting* album (Word).

CABIN DEVOTIONS: GOOD PLANS

As kids settle in their beds, invite them each to discuss the good things about sex and God's plan for it.

Ask:

● **Would you rather have the whole gift or just part of it?**

Follow up comments by explaining that waiting until marriage enables us to experience the whole gift—the uniting and exciting power of sex. Refusing to wait shortchanges us and each person we have sex with.

Read aloud Jeremiah 29:11. Invite kids to put the verse in their own words.

SATURDAY

SEALED ORDERS

Send kids each outside to a private place with their Bible, a pencil and an envelope containing their "Sealed Orders." Have them each study Bible passages about God's plan for sex.

After several minutes, call kids together and give them these answers to their "Sealed Orders": a—Hebrews 13:4; b—Proverbs 5:18-19; c—Genesis 2:23-25; and d—Genesis 1:28.

SESSION 2: MEDIA MESSAGES AND MYTHS

Sex Media Search—As kids enter the room, have them form groups of four to six. Guide groups each to stations stocked with a piece of posterboard, scissors, markers, masking tape, magazines,

Discover in the Bible God's great plan for sex! Write these Bible references next to the truth that describes them:

- Genesis 1:28
- Genesis 2:23-25
- Proverbs 5:18-19
- Hebrews 13:4

a. God created sex for marriage. ＿＿＿＿＿＿＿＿

b. God wants married couples to enjoy the pleasure of sex. ＿＿＿＿＿＿＿＿

c. God created women so men would find them attractive and men so women would find them attractive ("bone of my bones and flesh of my flesh!"). Sex is just one aspect of this attraction. ＿＿＿＿＿＿＿＿

d. God created sex for procreation (making babies). ＿＿＿＿＿＿＿＿

Spend time praying about God's plan for your marriage and how excited you are to experience his good gift in marriage. Ask him to help you wait.

album jackets, posters, tabloids and whatever else your kids read. Give kids each a copy of the "Media Search Instructions" and have them follow the instructions there.

When kids are finished, have groups each explain their poster. Give a round of applause for each message.

Identify the Myths—Have teams each pass their poster one station to the left. Give teams each two pieces of paper and a marker. Direct the teams to scan the posters for truths and myths and to write myths on one page and truths on the other. Again, challenge each team to discover more than other teams.

After five minutes, call for teams to tape their posters and papers to the wall. Invite junior highers to point out the most-important truths and most-believed myths.

Ask:

● **Why is it so important to pinpoint myths?**

After several suggestions, use kids' words to write on an overhead transparency a statement similar to this one: "Believing myths about sex or failing to understand truths about sex causes unhappiness."

God Made You Lovable—Say: **The best source for sexual truth is the creator of sex. Who is he? God himself. God has**

Media Search Instructions

Search your materials for messages about sex. They can be true or false. Copy the words or pictures onto your posterboard. Try to find more messages than any other team. You can "cheat" by adding messages not in your materials that you've heard from friends at school, or on favorite TV shows or videos.

created each of you as a sexual and lovable person.

Give junior highers each a credit-card-size piece of posterboard and a fine-tip marker. Have them each write this statement on the front side: "God created me a lovable person. He has given me sex to enjoy in marriage. I will honor and enjoy this gift."

Emphasize that God has given each junior higher considerable credit. Encourage kids to use this credit God's way.

Under-Chair Questions—Direct junior highers each to look under their chair for a Bible passage. Say: **Search your passage for at least one truth about sex. Put it in your own words.**

When everyone is finished, have kids each report their findings. Challenge kids each to write the truths on the back of their credit card, fitting as many as they can.

Say: **Following God's guidelines for sex helps you avoid many serious problems. To help you remember to follow God's guidelines for sex, keep the credit card in your billfold or wallet.**

Close with prayer.

SESSION 3: LINE LEVELERS

How vs. What—Review the previous session by inviting junior highers each to state one of God's truths about sex and why they like that truth. Tell kids they may "cheat" by looking at their credit cards. Ask:

● **Why don't we always live in God's truth?**

After several responses, say: **We have to discover ways to put his truth into practice. We do that by planning our response to myths about sex in actual dating situations. Myths often come to us as "come ons" or "lines"—what a date might say when he or she wants sexual affection.**

Line Crushers—Say: **Any time you're alone with someone of the opposite sex, especially someone you like, you're prone to be tempted sexually. Lines or pressure from that person make it even worse.**

Direct kids each to imagine being in a romantic situation with someone they really like. Hold up the sack of "Lines" and say: **Draw one line from the sack and state a good way to respond to it. For example, to respond to "Do you want to go to the bedroom?" you might say "No, my bedtime is much later."**

Go around the room and have kids each draw one line. Have them each read aloud their line and respond to it in turn. After each line is read, discuss how kids might respond wisely to the statement.

I Can Be Honest—Ask:

● **Why do people use lines?**
● **What can be done about them?**

Explain that lines are a form of dishonesty. Challenge junior highers each to name a way to be honest in relationships. Have kids each begin with the letter or sound of their first name. For example, a junior higher might say, "I'm **S**usan and I'll be honest by being **s**ensitive to feelings."

Sex Commercials—Say: **Advertisers continually exploit sex to sell their products. Now that you've discovered some myths and truths about sex, you can enjoy looking forward to sex without exploiting it. You can also advertise the beauty of God's plan for sex.**

Form groups of four to six. Have groups each create a commercial advertising the advantages of preparing for sex in marriage by following God's plan. Suggest they include ways to understand and live by God's plan.

Have groups each present their commercial.

Lines

Photocopy and cut apart these strips and place them in a paper sack. Make sure you have enough so each person can have one.

✂ -

● "If you love me, you'll let me."

✂ -

● "It hurts so much to not be able to make love to you."

✂ -

● "Everybody's doing it."

✂ -

● "You really want this. Let's go for it."

✂ -

● "If you stay this frigid, I can't stay with you."

✂ -

● "Let me make a real woman/man out of you."

✂ -

● "It's okay—we have birth control."

✂ -

● "Let's go into the bedroom."

✂ -

● "It's okay as long as we love each other."

✂ -

● "We're already married in God's eyes."

✂ -

● "This will make our love permanent."

✂ -

● "I want to give myself to you."

✂ -

● "You're so selfish not to do this for me."

✂ -

Redistribute the "Sex Handbook" and direct junior highers each to write on the second page of their handbook ways they'll respond to lines and ways they'll be honest. When kids are finished, collect the handbooks for use in a later session.

SHAVING CREAM FIGHT

Kids love shaving cream on a retreat. Organize the fight to start at a specific time, banning kids from the fight if they squirt even one dab beforehand. Choose a site where nothing will be damaged. Have non-fighters lead cheers or act as judges to determine who used the most creative fighting techniques and who has the most shaving cream on his or her body. See page 24 for more information on shaving cream fights.

SESSION 4: LOVE COUNSELOR

Prove Me Wrong—Say: **It's easier to talk about sexual limits than to establish and keep them.**

Play "devil's advocate" and name several reasons keeping sex within marriage is "old fashioned." For example, "We just want to show our love for each other" or "We're going to get married anyway." Challenge junior highers to prove you wrong

How to Say No Rounder—After the discussion, say: **We agree that God's plan brings greater happiness—not less. But statistics indicate that Christian teenagers—including many junior highers—are among those getting pregnant outside marriage.**

Ask:

● **Why do Christian teenagers have sex?**

● **How does deciding ahead of time not to have sex help you stop in the actual situation?**

Say: **One reason people have sex is that they each fear their sweetheart won't like them or will be hurt if they say no. They don't want to spoil the moment.**

Read aloud 1 Corinthians 10:13 and say: **Let's discover ways God might help us say no yet still help us preserve the romance.**

Gather everyone in a circle. Say: **Beginning with me, each of us will say one sentence or action that could stop sexual activity. Each person around the circle has 15 seconds to speak. If you can't think of anything to say when it's your turn, you must stand up. Then, if you think of one the next time around the circle, you may sit down.**

Use these examples to help kids who're having trouble thinking of anything:

- talk over convictions about sex beforehand;
- sneeze;
- say, "Let's learn to express our love other ways";
- move hands to safer areas; or
- say, "My parents would kill me."

Affirm students' wisdom. Then lead a prayer asking God for wisdom and firmness of conviction.

Here's My Problem—Give junior highers each paper and a pencil. Say: **Think about a love or sex situation you or a friend currently face. Write a "Dear Love Life Counselor" letter. Don't sign it. I'll collect and redistribute the letters to new owners who'll write responses.**

After a few minutes, collect, shuffle and redistribute the letters. Have junior highers each answer their letter using truths discovered during the retreat. Encourage honesty and sensitivity.

When everyone is finished, ask for volunteers to read aloud their letters and responses, being careful not to embarrass anyone.

Close with prayer.

POPCORN GAMES

Form teams by giving kids each a cut-out letter from the word "popcorn." Have kids each form groups by joining with others who have letters that complete the word. If you have extra kids, add them to groups already in process.

Have each team stay together for these popcorn games:

Mouth Stuff—Discover who can hold the most popped kernels in his or her mouth. The "mouth" cannot chew. One teammate counts while the others gently stuff. Provide a trash bag to deposit the "evidence" after the Mouth Stuff.

Popcorn Toss—Have team members each toss a popped kernel of corn across the room. Measure the distance of each team member's toss and add up all the distances. The team with the greatest *total* distance wins.

Kernel Race—Have teams relay against each other to carry the greatest number of unpopped kernels to a bowl at the opposite end of the room. Provide a spoon or knife to carry the kernels. The team with the greatest number of kernels in the bowl wins—*not* the first to complete the event.

Popcorn Sculptures—Have kids each work to create a sculpture with popped kernels and toothpicks. Affirm each junior higher by having kids each share their sculpture with their team and each team member tell what they like about each sculpture.

POPCORN SNACK

Serve popcorn with popcorn flavorings such as cheese, sour cream and salt. Serve fruit juices or soft drinks.

Tie into the theme by asking:
● **How is popcorn like sex?**
After kids respond, add: **It's not good if you try to eat popcorn before it's popped—like sex before marriage.**

CABIN DEVOTIONS: HANDBOOK REVIEW

Redistribute the "Sex Handbooks" and direct students each to write or doodle on the third page of their handbook ways to affirm and live God's good plan for sex. Read aloud scriptures such as Matthew 6:33 and Philippians 4:13. Say: **As you put God first, he'll meet your need for love, help you discover ways to express love without sex and give you the power to wait.**

Invite kids to talk about what they want in a love relationship. Affirm each dream and encourage kids to find God's best. Pray that God will prepare each teenager and future spouse for a beautiful relationship.

SUNDAY

CLOSING WORSHIP

Begin worship by singing a few of your group's favorite retreat songs. Then allow junior highers to share ways the retreat has affected them.

Guide kids to share on these topics:
● a person who's helped me grow this weekend and how;
● a discovery I've made that'll change my life; and
● an event or experience I want to thank God for.

Summarize the retreat's theme by thanking God for his good gift of sex. Invite them to add their own prayers of request and thanksgiving. Close by reading aloud Jeremiah 29:11.

Responding to Feelings

Emotions are great when we're up but the pits when we're down. Why do feelings seem to rule our lives—especially as young teenagers? What do feelings mean? What can we do about them? How does God speak through and help us with feelings?

This retreat helps kids recognize feelings as a part of the good way God created us and realize that feelings can be a way God communicates with us. It encourages balance between listening to feelings and being ruled by them.

OBJECTIVES

During this retreat junior highers will:
- determine emotions they feel and why they feel them;
- examine love, sadness, laughter and fear;
- discover that emotions are signals to respond to, not deny;
- explore ways to use emotions for good purposes; and
- let God help them with emotional struggles.

SUPPLY CHECKLIST

You'll need:
- ❑ 3×5 cards
- ❑ masking tape
- ❑ funny videos
- ❑ video equipment
- ❑ matches
- ❑ trash can
- ❑ large box
- ❑ three small square boxes that will all fit into the large box
- ❑ newsprint
- ❑ two sets of three different-shape balloons
- ❑ decorator icing

For each person you'll need:
- ❑ paper
- ❑ pen or pencil
- ❑ balloon
- ❑ Bible
- ❑ "How's My Love Life?" handout (page 106)
- ❑ envelope
- ❑ "Sealed Orders" handout (page 108)
- ❑ tissue
- ❑ marker
- ❑ cup of water
- ❑ "Seek God First" handout (page 111)
- ❑ plain round cookie
- ❑ small box

RETREAT PREPARATION

● **Love Is From God**—Inflate a balloon for each junior higher. Write one of the following questions each on a separate balloon: "Who do you like?" "Are you going with anyone?" "Have you talked to her?" "Did he ask you out yet?" "Who likes you?" and "Is it love?"

● **Snack and Together Games**—Have kids each bring snacks from home to share with the group.

● **Sealed Orders**—Make a copy of the "Sealed Orders" for each junior higher. Place each copy in a separate envelope.

● **Respond to the Message**—On separate 3×5 cards, write a different sadness category; for example, guilt, depression, loneliness, grief, discouragement, confusion. Make several cards for each category—enough so each person can have one. Tape one card to the bottom of each chair in the meeting room.

● **I Need All the Help I Can Get**—Write on separate 3×5 cards several things kids do to achieve happiness; for example, party, make friends, drink alcohol, have sex, get good grades, try to impress others.

● **What Do You Fear?**—Create a fear card for each person by writing different fears on separate 3×5 cards. Consider these examples: looking dumb, dying, family member dying, being rejected, being mugged, making a mistake, falling.

● **Perfect Love**—Before the activity, instruct someone to be ready on your cue to turn off the lights and make a loud crashing sound.

ON THE ROAD

Invite junior highers to tell a "feeling" story. For example, one teenager could begin by saying, "I was so depressed that ..." Then the next person could finish that sentence and start the next one to continue the story. For example: "... I went to my room and cried. I was crying because my boyfriend broke up with me over ..."

Encourage kids to change emotions from time to time.

THE RETREAT

FRIDAY

SESSION 1: HOW'S YOUR LOVE LIFE?

Emotional Beginning—As kids enter, give them each three slips of paper, and a pen or pencil. Have them each write a different emotion they feel on each piece of paper; for example, joy, happiness, depression, grief, anger, excitement, love. Collect the slips, shuffle them and use them to play Win, Lose or Draw.

Here's how to play:

1. Form teams of four or five. Give teams each several pieces of paper and a marker.

2. Have teams each designate an artist to start. Have artists come to you and look at an emotion from one of the slips kids wrote.

3. As soon as artists read the emotion, have them each run to their team and draw the emotion on paper on the floor. Artists may not speak. The first team to guess correctly must jump up as a group and shout the emotion. Award a million points for each correct answer. Rotate the job of artist among team members so everyone gets a chance to draw.

After the game, say: **On this retreat, we'll explore why we have these feelings and what to do about them. The four emotions we'll focus on are love, sadness, happiness and fear.**

RETREAT SCHEDULE

FRIDAY

8 p.m.	Session 1: How's Your Love Life?
9:30 p.m.	Welcome and Rule Reminders
9:45 p.m.	Snack and Together Games
11 p.m.	Cabin Devotions: God's Plan for Love

SATURDAY

8 a.m.	Breakfast
8:30 a.m.	Sealed Orders
9 a.m.	Session 2: Why Are You So Sad?
10:30 a.m.	Cluster Tag
Noon	Lunch
1 p.m.	Session 3: What's So Funny?
3 p.m.	Free Time
5 p.m.	Clean Up for Supper
6 p.m.	Supper
7 p.m.	Session 4: What Are You Afraid Of?
8:30 p.m.	Create Your Own Games
9:30 p.m.	Snack: Emotion Cookies
10 p.m.	Cabin Devotions: How God Speaks Through Emotions

SUNDAY

8 a.m.	Breakfast
8:30 a.m.	Closing Worship
9:30 a.m.	Leave for home!

Love Is From God—Bounce out the balloons with questions written on them. Have junior highers each grab one balloon as you say: **Questions like these seem to always be bouncing around in our minds.**

Ask:

● **Why are we so concerned about relationships with the opposite sex?**

● **Why do we yearn so strongly for love?**

Call for a volunteer to read aloud Jeremiah 17:9.

Ask:

● **How does Jeremiah describe the heart?**

● **How is the heart deceitful?**

● **How can we move from deceit to true love in our relationships?**

Encourage kids to find the answer in Jeremiah 17:7-8, 10. After several kids share, say: **God promises to check each heart and show the motives. God reveals what you place your security in, because he knows you can truly love others only when you place your security in God. Placing your security in God means finding your worth in him and relying on him to protect you.**

Ask:

● **What does Jeremiah compare security to?**

● **How does security affect love?**

● **Why does it make sense to grow our security roots deep in God?**

Love Test—Give kids each a Bible and have them look up 1 Corinthians 13. Give kids each a "How's My Love Life?" handout. Say: **You can decide to grow the kind of love life that brings both good feelings and strong relationships. Ultimately love is a decision.**

When everyone has finished, ask:

● **What was your total score?**

● **What actions could increase your score?**

● **Which areas do you think will be easiest to increase? hardest?**

● **How would the people you like score on this profile?**

SNACK AND TOGETHER GAMES

Before serving snacks, direct kids to stand shoulder to shoulder in a circle, facing inward. Have kids each reach into the center of the circle and grab one hand of two different people.

Challenge kids to untangle themselves without unclasping

How's My Love Life?

True love begins with feelings but continues with a decision. The love actions listed in 1 Corinthians 13:4-7 keep love growing. Circle a number in each line to rank how well you already love in these ways.

Impatient	1	2	3	4	5	6	7	8	9	10	Patient
Cruel	1	2	3	4	5	6	7	8	9	10	Kind
Envious	1	2	3	4	5	6	7	8	9	10	Secure
Proud	1	2	3	4	5	6	7	8	9	10	Humble
Rude	1	2	3	4	5	6	7	8	9	10	Considerate
Selfish	1	2	3	4	5	6	7	8	9	10	Cooperative
Easily angered	1	2	3	4	5	6	7	8	9	10	Talks out anger
Keeps record of wrongs	1	2	3	4	5	6	7	8	9	10	Forgives and forgets
Delights in evil	1	2	3	4	5	6	7	8	9	10	Sad about evil
Betrays others	1	2	3	4	5	6	7	8	9	10	Protects others
Suspicious	1	2	3	4	5	6	7	8	9	10	Trusting
Pessimistic	1	2	3	4	5	6	7	8	9	10	Hopeful
Quits	1	2	3	4	5	6	7	8	9	10	Perseveres

Scoring

0 to 49—Someone has deceived you! You're creating sadness rather than love.

50 to 99—Moving toward true love but still needing improvement.

100 to 130—You show great love potential. People will enjoy being your friend or sweetheart.

hands. After they succeed, say: **We can get into emotional knots without even meaning to. Getting out of predicaments seldom seems as easy, but with time and one move at a time, we can do it.**

Now serve snacks kids brought along and allow time for talking.

CABIN DEVOTIONS: GOD'S PLAN FOR LOVE

After kids pile into their bunks, ask:

● **How do you know if you're in love?**

After several comments, say: **Believing "you just know" is misleading. Love is more a commitment than a feeling.**

Ask:

● **What indicators reveal love in a relationship?**

● **If "love never fails" (1 Corinthians 13:8), then why do people divorce?**

SATURDAY

SEALED ORDERS

Have kids each take a Bible, pencil and an envelope containing their "Sealed Orders" to a private place outside.

After several minutes, bring kids back to the meeting place. Ask:

● **What did you learn during your Bible study?**

● **What are the advantages of letting your love roots grow in God?**

● **Why is it important to "fall in love" with someone who has the same roots?**

Pray that kids will have courage to seek love God's way.

SESSION 2: WHY ARE YOU SO SAD?

Feelings Are Messages—As kids enter, have them form a circle and hand them each a tissue and a marker. Say: **Write on the tissue actions, attitudes or events that make you sad.**

When kids are finished, have them each share what they wrote. Then have them each blow their tissue to the center of the circle.

Ask:

● **Is it a sin to be sad? Why or why not?**

● **Why does God allow sadness?**

SEALED ORDERS

You studied Jeremiah 17:7-10 last night as a group. Make its truths personal by completing the blanks according to verses 7 through 10 and then reading the passage to yourself.

7: Blessed am I when I trust in the _____, when my confidence is in him.

8: I will be like a _____ planted by the _____ that sends out its

_____ by the stream. I will not fear when _____ comes nor

will I have _____ in a year of drought. I will never fail to bear

_____.

For me this heat might be _____.
This drought might be _____.
This fruit might be _____.

9: My heart is _____ above all things and beyond _____.
I certainly can't understand it.

My heart is especially prone to deceit when
_____.

10: The _____ searches my heart and examines my _____.

He will _____ me according to my conduct and deeds.

This makes me want to act _____ and do
_____.

Have kids each grab the card you taped under their chair before the session. Say: **Read your sadness category and team up with others who have the same category.**

When kids are in their groups, say: **In your groups, respond to these questions about your sadness category:**

● **What might God be saying to us through this sad feeling?**
● **What could be its cause?**

Encourage team members to take turns naming causes and what they think God would want them to do about the feeling. For example, a junior higher might say: "I might be feeling guilty because I've neglected my friend. God wants me to apologize and spend more time with my friend."

I Don't Have to Stay Sad—Give kids each a Bible and have them look up John 4:4-45. Briefly tell the story of the woman at the well.

Then ask:

● **What did the woman in Samaria say about Jesus in John 4:29?**
● **What did she think this meant?**
● **How do you feel about Jesus knowing you inside and out?**
● **How might it give you security rather than fear?**

Say: **Jesus promised the Samaritan woman "living water." He wants to give it to you too.**

Give kids each a cup of water and have them each give it to the person on their left, saying, "Jesus wants to turn your sadness to joy."

Close with prayer.

CLUSTER TAG

Gather kids to play Cluster Tag. Set boundaries, then explain the rules: **One person is "It." When "It" tags someone, the tagged person runs with "It" to tag a third person. The cluster grows until "It" finally catches the last elusive victim.**

SESSION 3: WHAT'S SO FUNNY?

Laugh With Me, Not at Me—As junior highers enter, show funny videos such as football bloopers or Three Stooges pictures. Secure permission first.

Finding Security in God—After the videos, ask:
● **Can you picture God laughing? Why or why not?**
● **What do you think makes God laugh?**

● **What would make you truly happy?**

Call on several teenagers to talk for 30 seconds on what brings happiness. As kids each speak, write their main points on separate 3×5 cards.

When kids are finished, review the speeches using the cards. Pick out speeches that name unreliable sources of happiness. Read each card you picked out and illustrate how the item listed can fail to bring happiness. For example, if kids list "boyfriend," say: **A boyfriend gives happiness until he breaks up with you.**

Then tear the card in two and toss the pieces away. Or if kids list "possessions," say: **Possessions give happiness until they break, get lost or go out of style.**

Then use a match to set that card on fire.

Continue with other illustrations kids have given. Then pick up all the cards and hold them in a pile and say: **All these things together can give us happiness until some tragedy strikes.**

Drop the cards in a trash can. Then pick up a Bible and say: **But when our happiness is based in God, we have happiness that stays steady no matter what. And Matthew 6:33 explains that when we seek him first, all these other things will be added to us.**

Give kids each a "Seek God First" handout and a pencil, and have them each complete it.

When kids are finished, ask:

● **How have your relationships advanced God's kingdom? stifled it?**

● **What about your possessions? activities?**

On a large box write "Faith." Write "Friendships," "Romance" and "Possessions" each on separate smaller boxes.

Say: **Sometimes we see our Christian faith in one box, and our romances, friendships and possessions in other boxes. But our faith should encompass all the areas of our lives.**

Place each of the smaller boxes into the box labeled "Faith." Say: **Our faith holds all the parts of our lives together.**

I Know God Can Bring Happiness—Read aloud Luke 8:4-15. Ask:

● **What gets in the way of trusting God for our happiness?**

Give kids paper. Allow kids 30 seconds to list things they worry about.

After 30 seconds, read aloud Matthew 6:25-32. Say: **Because God knows our needs, we can turn our concerns over to him and wait for his direction.**

Seek God First

One way to seek God and his kingdom first (Matthew 6:33) is by noticing how certain possessions and relationships advance God's kingdom. Respond to these statements to see how your life advances God's kingdom.

1. My friendship with _____ advances God's kingdom by:

But it stifles God's kingdom by:

2. My romance with _____ advances God's kingdom by:

But it stifles God's kingdom by:

3. My clothes advance God's kingdom by:

But they stifle God's kingdom by:

4. My possessions advance God's kingdom by:

But they stifle God's kingdom by:

5. Spending time with _____ advances God's kingdom by:

But it stifles God's kingdom by:

I Need All the Help I Can Get—Give kids each one of the 3×5 cards with something kids do to find happiness written on it. Point out that some cards reveal good things and some bad. Say: **Look at your card and decide whether a Christian should do it.**

Have kids each respond. Allow other kids to disagree and discuss issues on the cards.

Have kids each lay their card in a pile in the center of the room. Lay a Bible on top of the pile.

Say: **There seem to be many ways to happiness, but only one way is true—God's way.**

Ask junior highers each to ask God about each area of their lives and let him guide them to happiness.

SESSION 4: WHAT ARE YOU AFRAID OF?

What Do You Fear?—As kids each enter, tape a fear card to their back. Say: **On your back is a card with a fear written on it. Find out your fear by asking "yes" or "no" questions. For example, you could ask, "Am I a person or a thing?" or "Have I happened before?"**

Encourage kids to look at each other's back and answer questions. When kids discover their identities, have them continue to help others find their identities.

Toward the end of the activity, secretly cue the person you talked to before the activity to turn out the lights and bang something loud, such as two trash can lids or two cooking pans.

After a few seconds, turn the lights on and gather everyone together.

Ask:
● **How did you feel?**
● **What's good about fear? bad?**
● **How was this fear good? bad?**

Have kids each name the fear on their back and tell whether the fear is good or bad. Have them explain their choice. Say: **Fear is natural, but can be destructive. God has an answer for bad fears.**

Read aloud 1 John 4:18. Form groups of four to six. Have kids each share one bad fear they have. Have group members suggest ways to overcome that fear with God's help.

Fear No More—Gather everyone together and have a volunteer read aloud 2 Timothy 1:7.

Ask:
● **What spirit has God *not* given us?**
● **What spirit has God given us?**

Write this equation on newsprint:

$$\text{Power} + \text{Love} + \text{Self-discipline} = \text{No Fear}$$

Ask these questions as you walk through the formula with kids:

● **How do some people use power?**
● **How would you define the power God gives us?**
● **How do some people use love to ease fear?**
● **How would you describe the love God gives us?**
● **How do some people use self-discipline to ease fear?**
● **How would you describe the self-discipline God gives us?**

Have kids get back into the groups they formed earlier. Say: **Name one of your bad fears and tell your group how power, love and self-discipline would ease that fear.**

Making a Response—Say: **We need to respond to our fears rather than deny them or let them control us.**

Ask:

● **How does denying fear harm you? others?**
● **How does letting fear control you harm you? others?**
● **How should you respond to fears?**
● **How does responding to fears help you? others?**

Have kids repeat these statements after you, one phrase at a time:

My emotions are good.
They come from God.
By understanding them
and responding to the needs behind them,
I can become more of the person God wants me to be.

CREATE YOUR OWN GAMES

Form two teams. Give teams each three different-shape balloons. Also give each team a sheet of newsprint and a marker. Say: **Invent a game all of us can play with your equipment. The game must be safe, fun and include everyone. Write how to play on your newsprint.**

Play the games.

After the games, congratulate kids' efforts. Say: **Working together we can find delightful ways to enjoy ourselves. We can also turn sadness into joy.**

SNACK: EMOTION COOKIES

Serve plain round cookies and provide decorator icing for kids to draw faces on their cookies.

After kids draw faces, ask:
● **What emotion does your cookie express?**
● **What makes your cookie feel that way?**
● **What advice would you give your cookie for dealing with that emotion?**

CABIN DEVOTIONS: HOW GOD SPEAKS THROUGH EMOTIONS

As the kids snuggle into their beds, have the cabin leader read aloud 2 Timothy 1:7. Share how God has spoken to you through emotions or has helped you through a rough time.

Ask:
● **When do you feel God most strongly?**
● **How do you know God is with you even when you can't feel him?**
● **What feeling has God helped you understand better during this retreat?**

SUNDAY

CLOSING WORSHIP

As kids enter, give each a small, square box and a marker. Say: **Write these emotions on different sides of the box: love, sadness, laughter and fear. On the other two sides, write two other emotions you experience.**

Have kids each set their box on the floor in front of them. Say: **Your emotions are part of the way God created you. Deuteronomy 6:5 and Luke 10:27 explain that God wants us to love him with all that we are.**

Have volunteers read aloud Deuteronomy 6:5 and Luke 10:27. Have kids each roll their box several times.

After each roll, ask:
● **How can you love God with the emotion showing on top of your box?**

Ask God to help kids see and respond to what he's telling them through their emotions.

Back-to-School Retreat

Back-to-school time is both anxious and exciting for junior high kids. They aren't sure what awaits them as new sixth-, seventh- or eighth-graders. Those who don't start at a new school will still start a new year and new challenges. The new year offers a fresh start, new teachers and new friends.

No one is more interested in kids' beginnings and challenges than God himself. But kids often miss this truth. They see church for weekends and school for "real life." This retreat guides junior highers to recognize God's care, and respond by inviting him to guide them through school. The retreat helps teenagers believe God cares and has the wisdom and power to handle any school situation.

This one-night retreat is designed to take place shortly before school starts. It could also be held during the school year by adapting discussion questions to address current rather than future concerns.

OBJECTIVES

During this retreat junior highers will:
- learn from other kids how to succeed in junior high;
- discover that God is intensely interested in school matters;
- identify ways to improve relationships with teachers;
- identify reasons for certain school courses;
- explore non-academic areas of school;
- equip each other to recognize and use their intelligence; and
- design ways to improve peer relationships.

SUPPLY CHECKLIST

You'll need:
❑ newsprint
❑ masking tape
❑ marker
❑ baking sheet
❑ salt

For every two people you'll need:
❑ paper cape
❑ set of markers

For each person you'll need:
❑ paper
❑ pencil
❑ Bible
❑ piece of black construction paper
❑ white chalk
❑ "Sealed Orders" handout (page 120)
❑ envelope
❑ picture of an infant or doll
❑ 3×5 card
❑ lump of cookie dough
❑ "Jesus' Recipe for Happiness" handout (page 125)

RETREAT PREPARATION

● **How to Succeed**—Secure three or four high schoolers—who've recently left junior high—to serve as a youth advisory board. Brief the panel on all they'll be required to do in the session.

● **Sealed Orders**—Make a copy of the "Sealed Orders" handout for each junior higher. Seal each copy in a separate envelope.

ON THE ROAD

As kids enjoy the bus or car ride, do scavenger hunts with wallets or purses. Prepare a list of items that may be found in a wallet or purse. Organize the hunt in one of these ways:

● Name one item at a time and have kids look for it. The first person to find it wins points.

● Form teams and give each team the list. The team to find the most items in a certain time wins.

THE RETREAT

FRIDAY

SESSION 1: ADVICE FROM THOSE WHO'VE BEEN THERE

No Laughing Matter—As junior highers enter, guide them through a game of Ha Ha. Have the first junior higher lie on the floor near and parallel to the wall. Have the second person lay his or her head on the first person's stomach so the two of them form a "T." The third person lays his or her head on the second person's stomach. Continue until everyone lies on someone else's stomach forming a zigzag.

In sequence, have kids each say "ha" according to where they are in the sequence. For example, the first person would say "ha," the second person would say "ha, ha," the third person would say "ha, ha, ha," and so on.

Say: **The object is to get all the way to the end without anyone adding any more ha's than his or her position.**

Start over every time someone laughs or adds too many ha's. Continue until the group succeeds.

Ask:
● **What did you find difficult about this experience? easy?**
● **Was this experience fun? Why or why not?**
● **How is this experience like school? unlike school?**

Say: **Just as you had to be self-controlled and alert to succeed at the game, so you have to use self-control to keep up with the fast pace of school.**

How to Succeed—Introduce your youth advisory team, composed of kids who've recently left junior high and are now in high school. Include at least one affirming characteristic about each. Say: **These advisers have been where you're going. They'll share tips for success in junior high and then answer your questions.**

Format the discussion like a daytime TV talk show. Give junior highers each three slips of paper and a pencil, and have them each write three school questions for the panel. Say: **You might want to ask about topics such as what to do when I don't know anyone in class, what panelists wish they had or had not done while they were in junior high, how to discover what a teacher wants or how to get along with difficult teachers.**

Say to the panel: **Let's have each of you share three tips for success in junior high.**

RETREAT SCHEDULE

FRIDAY

7 p.m.	Session 1: Advice From Those Who've Been There
9 p.m.	Depart for Retreat Site
11 p.m.	Snack and Rule Reminders
11:30 p.m.	Cabin Devotions: How God Helps Me at School

SATURDAY

8 a.m.	Breakfast
8:30 a.m.	Sealed Orders
9 a.m.	Session 2: Super Teachers
10:30 a.m.	Free Time
11:30 a.m.	Lunch
12:30 p.m.	Session 3: Why Do We Have to Learn All This Stuff?
2 p.m.	Free Time
4:30 p.m.	Clean Up for Supper
5 p.m.	Supper
6:30 p.m.	Session 4: Relationships Count Too
8 p.m.	Snack, Singing and Sharing
9 p.m.	Closing Worship
10 p.m.	Head for Home

After panelists share, invite kids to ask their questions. Have questions ready to ask in case discussion lags. After the discussion, thank the panelists and give them a chance to offer any final words of advice.

God Cares About Junior High—Ask junior highers:
● **On a scale of 1 to 10, how concerned do you think God is about your school worries? your school successes? Why?**
Say: **The Bible teaches that God's interested in the details of our lives.**

Have a volunteer read aloud Psalm 139:1-12. Then assign each verse to a different junior higher. Give kids each paper and a pencil, and have them each rewrite their verse, personalizing it and applying it to their school life.

When everyone's finished, have kids read aloud their verses in order.

Bring It to the Light—Give kids each black construction paper. Say: **Using your pencil, write the school problem you're most worried about right now.**

When kids are finished, distribute white chalk and say: **Now use your chalk to write this sentence across that problem: "God understands and will show me what to do."**

Read aloud Psalm 139:11-12. Have kids offer sentence prayers, sharing their school worries with God.

CABIN DEVOTIONS: HOW GOD HELPS ME AT SCHOOL

As kids settle into bed, invite them each to share one way Jesus helps them at school. Encourage them to share favorite Bible verses.

SATURDAY

SEALED ORDERS

As breakfast ends, have junior highers each take a Bible, pencil and their "Sealed Orders" to a private place outside.

After several minutes call kids back to the meeting area and ask:
● **What did you learn during your Bible study?**
● **How can you apply it to your life?**
Read aloud Psalm 139 as a prayer to close the discussion.

You studied Psalm 139:1-12 last night as a group. Make its truths personal by reading each verse and completing the sentences that follow.

Verse 1
Lord I don't like it that you know . . .

But I'm glad you know . . .

Verse 2
God, you understand that at school I think . . .

Verse 3
Lord, you're familiar with my way of _____ at school.

Verse 4
Before I say it, God, you know I want to say . . .

Verse 5
This verse makes me feel secure because . . .

Verse 6
God, your knowledge of me amazes me because . . .

Verses 7-8
It's great to know that no matter where I go, you're with me Lord. I especially need you when . . .

Verses 9-10
I love knowing you'll guide me, God. Right now I most want your guidance for . . .

Verse 11
Lord, the area of greatest darkness in my life right now is . . .

Verse 12
Lord, I need you to light up this darkness by . . .

SESSION 2: SUPER TEACHERS

Enter Super Teacher—As junior highers enter, have them form pairs. Give pairs each a paper cape and a set of markers. Say: **Write on your cape a logo or description of the perfect teacher.**

Have pairs each explain their creation.

After each presentation, ask:

● **Why do these characteristics make a super teacher?**

● **What prevents all teachers from being this good?**

Give kids each paper and a pencil. Say: **Write a description of a teacher you had who was less than super. Use no names or identifying details. Title your page "Not-So-Super Teacher."**

Collect these without names to use later in the session.

Decide to Learn—Have a volunteer read aloud Romans 13:1-7 as the others follow in their Bibles. Write each of the following on a separate sheet of newsprint: Strongly Agree, Agree, Disagree or Strongly Disagree. Tape the four sheets of newsprint each to a different wall.

Say: **I'll make a series of statements about this Bible passage. When I make a statement, go to the sign that tells how you feel about it.**

Read aloud the statements one at a time. After kids choose their positions, have them each comment on why they chose the position they did. Here are the statements:

● **All teachers are placed by God.**

● **Submitting to someone means respecting him or her.**

● **It's easier to respect and work with a teacher when you realize you're doing it for the Lord.**

● **God wants you to submit to all teachers, even those who don't obey him.**

● **Even when the teacher's wrong, rebelling can cause problems.**

● **If you do the right thing, you won't get in trouble at school.**

● **I owe my teachers respect and honor.**

● **God wants me to love my teachers.**

My Actions Affect My Teacher—Invite kids each to tell one way they might turn a not-so-super teacher into a super teacher.

Ask:

● **What's the difference between bringing out the best in a teacher and manipulating him or her?**

Distribute the "Not-So-Super Teacher" descriptions so their original writers don't have them. Say: **On the back of your page,** write advice for turning your "not-so-super teacher" into the "super teacher" described on our capes.

After several minutes, have kids each read their description and report their advice.

Close with a prayer for the teachers kids will have this fall.

SESSION 3: WHY DO WE HAVE TO LEARN ALL THIS STUFF?

What Would You Teach?—As junior highers enter, give each a picture of an infant or a doll. Form groups of four to six. Give groups each newsprint and markers. Say: **On your newsprint, list all the things your baby will have to know by the time he or she is 18.**

When groups finish, have them each share their list. Gather everyone together and say: **This is what schools try to do for us— prepare us for the real world.**

Ask:

● **How well do you think they're doing?**
● **Which courses help the most? Why?**
● **Which courses seem meaningless? Why?**

Look for a Reason—Have kids each read Proverbs 9:9-12. After kids each read the passage, ask the following questions one at a time. After you read each question, have kids stand as soon as they find the answer. Call on the first one standing. Ask these questions:

● **Can you ever know everything in this life?**
● **What's the beginning of wisdom? Why?**
● **What happens to people who fear the Lord?**
● **What happens if you mock or reject the Lord and his teachings?**

Say: **Not everything we learn in school is from the Lord, nor does it seem related to life. But much of it is. Let's find out how.**

Give kids each a 3×5 card and a pencil. Guide kids each to write on their card a subject or teaching at school that seems foolish or useless. Have kids barter with each other for the items listed on their cards. Encourage kids to trade subjects they don't want for those they value more.

After kids have made several trades, call everyone together and say: **What one person can't use, another can. For example, someone might hate math but love Spanish, so he or she trades with a person who loves math but hates Spanish. One person's junk is another's treasure.**

Ask:

● **How does studying even uninteresting subjects increase your wisdom? your faith?**

What I Want to Learn—On a sheet of newsprint, write these problems: radioactive waste disposal, pollution, poverty, war, vandalism, disease, hunger, drug abuse, crime, gangs, alcoholism, AIDS.
Ask:
● **What subjects and specifics might you need to know to solve these problems?**
Write kids' responses on newsprint.
After kids respond, ask:
● **Who'd like to commit themselves to learning something this year that'll make a difference in the world?**
Have kids who raise their hands stand up. As a group, pray for God to strengthen them to fulfill their commitment.

SESSION 4: RELATIONSHIPS COUNT TOO

Cookie Creations—As kids enter, give them each a lump of cookie dough and instruct them to shape it into a cookie that depicts a role they play at school. For example, someone might fashion a band member, soccer halfback or a student council member.
Collect cookies on a baking sheet and place them in the oven to bake.
While the cookies are baking, form teams of four or fewer and have kids play School Charades. Have teams each come up with two or three school items to imitate. Use these examples to help teams think of items: textbook, stairway, desk, ruler, teacher, principal, pencil, backpack, locker. Explain that each team member must participate in each charade done by his or her team. Have teams take turns presenting their charades while other teams guess. Applaud each team's attempts.
After taking the cookies from the oven, have kids each explain their cookie.
Ask:
● **What do you like about your role?**
● **What do you not like about it?**
● **How might you serve God through that role?**

How to Be Happy—Ask:
● **How do sports make you happy?**
● **How do friendships make you happy?**
● **How does belonging to a school club make you happy?**
Say: **Happiness is an important concern. Jesus taught nine**

ways to be happy in Matthew 5. Look in Matthew 5:3-10 to discover what word each verse starts with.

Ask:

● **What does "blessed" mean?**

Give junior highers each a copy of "Jesus' Recipe for Happiness" and assign one ingredient to each junior higher. Have them each apply the beatitudes to their life in relation to sports, friends or school activities. When kids are finished, have them report what they wrote.

I Can Make Others Happy Too—Say: **One reason school makes us worry is we want to look smart. There are many kinds of smart. For example, book smart, social smart, mechanical smart, creativity smart and athletic smart. This group possesses all these kinds.**

Stand behind each junior higher and invite the group to call out ways that person is smart.

Salt Lick—Have a volunteer read aloud Matthew 5:13-16. Say: **Salt makes people thirsty to meet Jesus and to serve him. Light reveals the true nature of things and allows people to see clearly.**

Pour salt in each junior higher's hand and have kids each taste it. Say: **As the taste lingers through the evening, ask God which salt or light action he most wants you to do at school this year.**

SNACKING, SINGING AND SHARING

As kids eat a snack, invite them to talk about one or more of the areas listed below. Between topics, sing a song about God's daily provision such as "He's Everything to Me." Sharing topics include:

● a specific way I feel more ready for school this fall;
● a way I'll encourage my friends at school;
● something God has taught me about school;
● a relationship I'll work on at school (peer or adult);
● a praise about school;
● a praise for someone here on the retreat; and
● a praise for something that's happened between God and me this weekend.

CLOSING WORSHIP

Build your worship around Psalms 136—137. Form teams of two or three and give them each paper and a pencil. Direct teams each to write Psalm 137 in their own words as it relates to school sadness and

Jesus' Recipe for Happiness

Complete each ingredient for happiness by telling how to mix it with sports, friends, band or other school activities. Look in the second half of each verse of Matthew 5:3-10 for a hint and think about how Jesus would teach this principle in your school.

Add one cup of poorness in spirit, which means: (v. 3)

_____

_____

When mourning starts look for comfort which means: (v. 4)

_____

_____

Sprinkle meekness by: (v. 5)

_____

_____

A generous portion of hunger and thirsting for righteousness can be added by: (v. 6)

_____

_____

Stirring relationships with mercy will cause you to: (v. 7)

_____

_____

Pour all the above into a pure heart to ensure: (v. 8)

_____

_____

Fold peacemaking into your relationships in order to: (v. 9)

_____

_____

When the heat of persecution comes because of righteousness: (v. 10)

_____

_____

frustrations. To help kids write their psalm, ask:

● **What makes you feel captive at school?**
● **Who are your captors?**
● **Who makes fun of your faith?**

Have groups read aloud their Psalm 137 paraphrases.

Say: **God can help us handle these problems like he helped the Israelites. God helped them see they could be happy in any circumstance. Rewrite Psalm 136 to show how God can make you happy in both your smooth and rough school situations.**

Have groups read their Psalm 136 paraphrases as a closing prayer.

SECTION 3:

Junior High Lock-Ins

Building My Own Faith

Junior highers have questions about God and their faith. But they're sometimes afraid to ask their questions because they think such questions are bad or make them look weak. This lock-in encourages kids to explore their faith questions. It presupposes that asking God questions shows you trust him to have the answers. This lock-in explores God's existence, finds truths about him in the Bible, examines the reality of his love and demonstrates why the life he offers beats any other

OBJECTIVES

During this lock-in junior highers will:
- examine characteristics of God;
- realize questions can be a sign of faith—not denial of it;
- discover several reasons we know God is real;
- pinpoint solid ways to overcome their specific doubts;
- debunk misconceptions of God's love; and
- specify reasons the Christian life is the best option.

SUPPLY CHECKLIST

You'll need:
❏ 3×5 cards
❏ small nails
❏ hammer
❏ block of ice
❏ "hollow" and "solid" snacks
❏ two copies of "Love Skit" (page 137)
❏ paper sack
❏ background music
❏ stereo
❏ masking tape
❏ newsprint
❏ scissors
❏ trumpet
❏ breakfast supplies
❏ helium tank

For each person you'll need:
❏ pencil
❏ Bible
❏ "Go to the Source" handout (pages 133 and 134)
❏ paper
❏ marker
❏ balloon
❏ pen

LOCK-IN PREPARATION

● **Dash Doubts**—Prepare a block of ice by freezing a gallon milk carton filled with water. Cut the carton away before the activity.

● **Respond to Love With Love**—Before the lock-in, enlist two junior highers to act out the "Love Skit." Provide each actor with a copy of the script.

THE LOCK-IN

CROWDBREAKER: PASSWORD

As kids come in, give each a pencil and a 3×5 card. Have kids each write one word describing God. Explain that this is their entry ticket.

When everyone has arrived, collect tickets and involve kids in a game of Password using the words they wrote on their cards. Form teams of five—two sets of partners and one moderator—and divide the tickets among the moderators. Review the rules of Password:

LOCK-IN SCHEDULE

8 p.m.	Crowdbreaker: Password
8:30 p.m.	Introduction and Overview of Rules
8:45 p.m.	Session 1: How Do I Know God Is Real?
9:45 p.m.	Snack Break: Look Inside
10:15 p.m.	Session 2: Does God Really Love Me?
11:15 p.m.	Exercise Break: Calisthenics
11:30 p.m.	Session 3: Is the Christian Life Worth It?
12:30 a.m.	Perception Games
1:30 a.m.	Free Time
2:30 a.m.	Early Bird Snack
3 a.m.	Everybody Sleeps
6:30 a.m.	Rise and Shine Race
7 a.m.	Breakfast and Cleanup
7:30 a.m.	Closing Worship
8 a.m.	Head for Home

1. Sit facing your partner and next to your opponent.

2. Your leader will show you and your opponent a characteristic of God. The person with a birthday nearest to Christmas goes first. This person gives a one-word clue to his or her partner to help the partner guess the characteristic. If successful, the pair gets 10 points. If unsuccessful, the opponent gives a one-word clue to his or her partner for nine points.

3. Continue to alternate giving clues until the characteristic is guessed or point value is zero.

4. Alternate sides and first-clue givers so each player gets to go first once every four rounds.

5. Your leader will keep score and be the final judge of whether the guess is correct.

After the game, call everyone together and ask:

● **How many characteristics can you remember from the game?**

● **What's your favorite characteristic of God? Why?**

● **Are any characteristics we named not really true of God? Explain.**

SESSION 1: HOW DO I KNOW GOD IS REAL?

Am I Bad if I Doubt?—To demonstrate that asking questions leads to answers, play a game of Twenty Questions. Say: **We'll take turns pretending to be an animal, a famous person or a thing. You may answer up to 20 "yes" or "no" questions to reveal your identity.**

Form groups of four. Have group members each take turns being the pretender, while other group members ask up to 20 "yes" or "no" questions. Kids may try to guess the pretender's identity as often as they want.

After group members each have had a turn as the pretender, call everyone together and ask:

● **How did we find each other's identity?**
● **How do questions lead to understanding?**
● **How might questions about God lead to deeper faith?**

Say: **Doubts or questions about God's existence are bad only when we leave them as doubts. When our doubts and questions motivate us to find and understand God, they spur us on to a deeper faith.**

Check Him Out—Give kids each a Bible and a copy of the "Go to the Source" handout. Form pairs and challenge kids to work together to complete the crossword puzzle before any other pair.

Encourage kids to look in their Bibles for the answers. Review the puzzle by inviting different pairs to give an answer to each blank. Ask:

● **How do these truths answer your questions about God?**
● **What other questions do you have about God?**

Address kids' questions with the group's help as best you can, volunteering to research any you can't answer.

Evidence Abounds—Say: **We just learned several characteristics of God and found evidence for our faith in the Bible.**

Ask:

● **How do we know someone didn't just make up God?**

After reading each item—one at a time—from the following list, have kids tell how each shows God is real:

● people;
● Bible;
● good;
● sense of right and wrong;
● personal experience;
● creation; and
● Jesus.

Go to the Source

The Bible is the source for answers about God. Practice finding answers in the Bible with this crossword puzzle. The answers are from the New International Version.

God's Existence

A. We know God is real because his qualities have been revealed since the ___(1)___ of the world (Romans 1:20).

B. God's eternal ___(2)___ and ___(3)___ nature can be understood by looking at what God has ___(4)___ (Romans 1:20).

C. God made us in such a way that we can ___(5)___ out for him and ___(6)___ him (Acts 17:27).

D. God is not ___(7)___ from any one of us (Acts 17:27).

Continued

God's Ways

E. When we ___(8)___, ___(9)___ or ___(10)___ we'll receive what we need from God (Luke 11:9-10).

F. Some people get mad at God because bad things happen to someone they love. But Matthew 5:45 explains that when bad things happen it doesn't mean God is at fault or that he's mad at you. God sends both rain and sun to both ___(11)___ and ___(12)___ people. In fact, God offers Christians his power to help them through the rough times. James 1:16-17 further explains that God is the giver of good and ___(13)___ gifts—not bad ones.

G. Other people deny God because they think he wants to take away all their fun. John 10:10 explains that God wants to give us ___(14)___ to the ___(15)___.

God's Gift of Salvation

H. Some people reject God because some Christians are hypocritical. Romans 7:18 explains that even Christians still have a ___(16)___ nature. Looking to Jesus, rather than sinful Christians, gives a better picture of God.

I. God gets upset about hypocrites too. James 1:22 explains that true religion is to not just ___(17)___ to God's Word but to ___(18)___ what it says.

J. Some people reject God because they feel they can't change. They fear the temptations will be too great, so they give up. First Corinthians 10:13 explains that God is ___(19)___ and will give us the power to resist temptation.

K. Some people reject God and the church because they feel unwanted or unneeded. First Corinthians 12:21-26 explains that every person is like a ___(20)___ of the body, and every part is ___(21)___ .

L. Some people reject God because they feel they're doing okay as they are. Romans 3:10 explains that because no one is ___(22)___ , we all need God.

M. Some people reject God because they feel they don't need what he has to offer. But we all need love, purpose, companionship and happiness. Philippians 4:19 explains that God can meet all these needs through ___(23)___ ___(24)___ . Matthew 6:33 explains that when we put God and his kingdom first, all these other things will be ___(25)___ as well.

Go to the Source Answer Key

After kids respond, ask:
● **What evidence convinces you that God is real? Why?**
● **What evidence seems hollow to you? Why?**

Dash Doubts—Ask:
● **Why do people doubt God is real?**

Invite kids to share personal doubts they have or doubts they know other people have. Write kids' responses on 3×5 cards and nail the cards to the block of ice.

As the block of ice starts to crack with each nailing, ask:
● **What evidence would dash these doubts?**

As kids each name a way to dash doubt, have them break away a cracked piece of the ice block. Say: **Just addressing the doubts with our hammer started to break the coldness. Finding an-**

swers broke it even further. But ice chips still remain.
Ask:
● **What could melt away this coldness?**
Say: **Warmth chases away coldness. As you receive Christ's love for you and others, you'll see God work in and through you. And as others experience God's warmth through you, he'll melt the ice in their hearts and give them new life.**

SNACK BREAK: LOOK INSIDE

Serve snacks, some of which are hollow on the inside and some of which are solid. For example, you could serve hollow and solid chocolate figures or sopapillas and brownies.

As kids eat, say: **Things aren't always as they seem. Sometimes things that seem full are really empty.** Ask:
● **How can you tell whether claims people make about Christ are hollow?**

Encourage kids to discover truth about God for themselves. Explain that truths about God can stand up under questions.

SESSION 2: DOES GOD REALLY LOVE ME?

Demonstrations of God's Love—Say: **I'm going to read a series of statements. After I read each statement, indicate how you feel about it by:**
● **standing if you strongly agree;**
● **sitting in a chair if you agree;**
● **sitting on the floor if you disagree; or**
● **lying on the floor if you strongly disagree.**
Read aloud these statements:
● **If you sin too much, God will love you less.**
● **God loves some people more than other people.**
● **Some people have done so many wrong things God can't love them anymore.**
● **It's easier to feel God's love at a lock-in than in everyday life.**
● **God loves me.**
Read aloud John 3:16. Say: **God loves each of us whether we *feel* loved or not. He sees what we can be and moves us toward that goal.**

Respond to Love With Love—Call on the previously enlisted pair of junior highers to present their "Love Skit."

After the skit, ask:

● **Who do you agree with more? Why?**

● **Why is obedience a logical reaction to God's love?**

Read aloud Micah 6:8.

Ask:

● **What other responses to his love does God want?**

● **How will you live out these responses in your daily life?**

I Seek and I Find—Read aloud Luke 11:9-10. Give kids each paper and a pencil. Say: **Write one question you'd like to ask God.**

Collect the questions in a paper sack. Guide kids to help each other find answers to their questions by playing Hot Bag. Have junior highers pass the bag of questions while music plays and stop when the music stops. Have the person holding the bag draw out a question and answer it as well as possible. Then have him or her invite more ideas from the group. If kids come up with a question no one can answer, research the answer later.

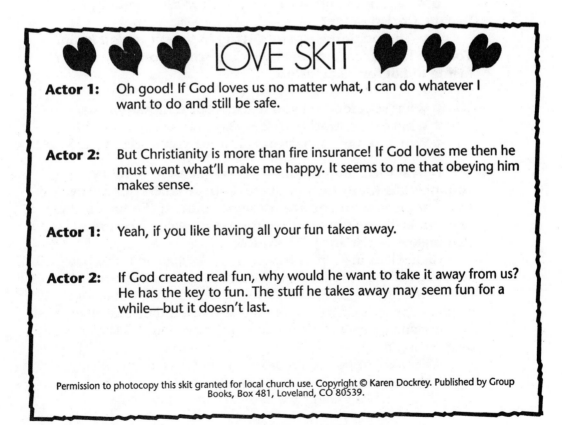

LOVE SKIT

Actor 1: Oh good! If God loves us no matter what, I can do whatever I want to do and still be safe.

Actor 2: But Christianity is more than fire insurance! If God loves me then he must want what'll make me happy. It seems to me that obeying him makes sense.

Actor 1: Yeah, if you like having all your fun taken away.

Actor 2: If God created real fun, why would he want to take it away from us? He has the key to fun. The stuff he takes away may seem fun for a while—but it doesn't last.

EXERCISE BREAK: CALISTHENICS

To wake kids up and keep their blood flowing, lead exercises. After the exercises, say: **Daily exercise makes you strong. Similarly, walking daily by faith strengthens your relationship with God.**
Ask:

● **How can you get started if you're spiritually flabby?**

SESSION 3: IS THE CHRISTIAN LIFE WORTH IT?

The Appeal of the Competition—Tape a super-size sheet of newsprint to the wall. Give junior highers each a marker and say: **Draw your own magazine ad for temptation. It can be a specific temptation, such as cheating, or simply a general appeal for giving in to temptation.**

When everyone is finished, have kids each explain their ad.
Ask:

● **Why didn't everyone draw a little man in a red suit with a pitchfork?**

● **Why don't more people live God's way?**

● **What does temptation have to do with whether people live the Christian life?**

Say: **Temptation isn't sin. Giving in to temptation is sin. You can keep from sinning by recognizing temptation and refusing to fall for its delusion.**
Ask:

● **What schemes did you use in your temptation ads?**

● **What other strategies does the devil use?**

● **Which temptations are easiest for you to resist? hardest?**

Defeat the Competition—Say: **People who write TV commercials know how to make their products appealing. You wrote some convincing ads for temptation at the start of this session. Let's use the same techniques to write a commercial that makes Christianity irresistible.**

Gather kids in a circle. Have kids each stand and state one advantage of the Christian faith; for example, security, friendship, understanding, belonging, true love. No one can use another person's answer. Give kids each 15 seconds to answer. If they can't, they must remain standing until you come around to them again. Then have them try again.

Write kids' responses on 3×5 cards and drop them into the "hot bag" from Session 2. When everyone has given an advantage, pass around the "hot bag" and have kids each draw one card.

Say: **Now write a commercial that advertises the advantage listed on your card. Remember to show why the Christian faith is worth living.**

When everyone's finished, have kids present their commercial. Encourage kids to applaud each commercial.

Choose to Believe—As a closing, have kids each take turns completing each of these sentences:

● I believe that God . . .
● I believe that Jesus . . .
● I'll show my faith by . . .
● I know God cares about me because . . .
● I believe the Christian life is worth living because . . .

PERCEPTION GAMES

Perception games are simple games that require you to look at things a certain way in order to play. One example is Crossed/Uncrossed, in which kids sit in a circle and pass around a pair of scissors saying "crossed" or "uncrossed" as they pass the scissors. The object is to discover when to say "crossed" and when to say "uncrossed." One or two are told in advance that the secret is whether the passer's legs are crossed or uncrossed. Most will incorrectly watch the manipulation of the scissors to discover the clue.

Another example is called the Bang Bang Game. In this game, the leader points his or her finger at several people in the room while saying, "bang, bang, bang" (or "bang, bang, bang, bang"—the number of times the leader says "bang" is unimportant). The leader then asks, "Who'd I shoot?" Kids must figure out how the leader determines who he or she shot. The secret is that the imaginary bullet falls on the first person to speak after the leader asks who was shot.

After the games, say: **Just as you had to watch closely and think during these games, sometimes you have to watch your life closely and think about God's Word to see why God's way of living makes more sense than any other way.**

RISE AND SHINE RACE

Rouse the slumbering with "reveille" from an actual trumpet, if available. Challenge kids to clean up in trios, rewarding the first trio to breakfast with a prize, such as letting the winners be first in line. Before serving breakfast, make sure everyone has dressed, packed and cleaned his or her room.

BREAKFAST AND CLEANUP

Let your breakfast continue the faith theme by spelling it out with food. Serve these "faith" courses one at a time:
- F—for fried eggs;
- A—for apple juice;
- I—for iced donuts;
- T—for toast; and
- H—for ham, hot chocolate or hotcakes.

CLOSING WORSHIP

Hold this service outside if possible. Give junior highers each a balloon and a pen. Have them each blow up their balloon but not tie it off. Have them each write on their balloon one way they understand God and their faith better as a result of this lock-in. As they finish, have them come to the helium tank you've set out. Inflate each balloon with helium and tie it off. Have kids each let their balloon go with a prayer of thanks and a commitment to live by faith.

After everyone has released a balloon, call kids together and ask:
- **What did you write on your balloons?**
- **How do you feel closer to God now than before this lock-in?**
- **What do you understand better about God?**
- **How will your understanding make a difference in your everyday life?**

Encourage kids each to grow in their own personal faith—a faith that makes a difference both now and in eternity. Hug kids as they leave.

Discovering and Using My Spiritual Gifts

"I wish I could be like Leonard. He can do it all."

"I'd love for God to use me, but I can't do anything well."

Comments like these remind us that kids really do care about serving in church. God knows this and equips every Christian with one or more spiritual gifts. Each Christian, regardless of age, is important to the full functioning of the body of Christ.

This lock-in, based on 1 Corinthians 12:12—13:3, guides kids to pinpoint one or two gifts that might be theirs and challenges them to express their gifts in their daily lives.

OBJECTIVES

During this lock-in junior highers will:
- experience working together;
- dramatize body life;
- distinguish spiritual gifts from talents;
- pinpoint one or more spiritual gifts God may have given them; and
- help each other pinpoint and use their spiritual gifts.

SUPPLY CHECKLIST

You'll need:
- ❏ bed sheet
- ❏ set of six to eight Lego pieces—identical to the ones kids use
- ❏ newsprint
- ❏ 3×5 cards
- ❏ "Jolly Joints Strips" (page 148)
- ❏ several decks of playing cards
- ❏ bag of balloons

For each person you'll need:
- ❏ "Gift Hunt" handout (page 144)
- ❏ pencil
- ❏ Bible
- ❏ "Body Act" handout (page 146)
- ❏ paper
- ❏ "Gift Grading" handout (pages 150 and 151)
- ❏ "Gift-Shape Card" (page 154)
- ❏ marker

For every two people you'll need:
- ❏ one or more gift descriptions from the "Gift Grading" handout (pages 150 and 151)
- ❏ scissors
- ❏ masking tape
- ❏ box
- ❏ bow

For every four people you'll need:
- ❏ identical set of six to eight Lego pieces

LOCK-IN PREPARATION

● **Gift Hunt**—Before kids arrive, write each answer to the "Gift Hunt" handout on a separate 3×5 card. Hide the cards according to the directions on the handout. Here are the answers: 1. Holy Spirit; 2. every Christian; 3. encourager, giver, leader, mercy-giver, evangelist, pastor and teacher; 4. Romans 12, 1 Corinthians 12 and Ephesians 4.

● **Putting It Together**—Create a Lego structure using the Lego parts you have. Hide the structure behind a bed sheet and place the other sets of the Lego pieces in separate piles on the opposite side of the room.

● **Brief Break**—As part of their admission cost, have kids each bring a snack such as chips, cookies or soft drinks to share with the group.

● **Lists of Gifts**—Photocopy "Gift Grading" and cut apart the gifts. Make enough copies so each pair can have one gift description.

● **Stretch Break**—Photocopy "Jolly Joints Strips" and cut apart the strips into two separate decks. Shuffle each deck, then set aside.

● **Nothing Without Love**—Before the lock-in, enlist four or five junior highers to bring their band instruments with them. Have them be ready to play together out of tune.

LOCK-IN SCHEDULE

7:45 p.m.	Crowdbreaker: Gift Hunt
8 p.m.	Session 1: What Good Am I?
9:30 p.m.	Introductions
9:45 p.m.	Brief Break
10 p.m.	Session 2: What's a Spiritual Gift?
11 p.m.	Stretch Break
11:30 p.m.	Session 3: What's My Gift?
12:30 a.m.	Singing and Sharing
1 a.m.	Rotating-Partner Games
3 a.m.	Everybody Sleeps
6:30 a.m.	Arise and Eat!
7:30 a.m.	Closing Worship
8 a.m.	Head for Home

THE LOCK-IN

CROWDBREAKER: GIFT HUNT

As junior highers enter, give them each a copy of the "Gift Hunt" and a pencil. Challenge them each to complete the hunt without leaving the meeting room.

When everyone has completed the hunt, have volunteers each read one of these Bible passages taken from the chapters in #4 of the "Gift Hunt": Romans 12:6-8; 1 Corinthians 12:7-11; and Ephesians 4:11-13.

Ask:
● **What did you discover on your hunt?**
● **Why does God give Christians spiritual gifts?**

Gift Hunt

1. For the giver of spiritual gifts, look under a windowsill.

   _____

2. For the receiver of at least one spiritual gift, look on someone's back.

   _____

3. For seven samples of spiritual gifts look under several chairs.

   _____

   _____

   _____

4. For three Bible chapters that teach about spiritual gifts, look on the ceiling.

   _____

   _____

   _____

SESSION 1: WHAT GOOD AM I?

Putting It Together—Form teams of four. Assign each team member a different label: Eyes, Ears, Feet or Hands.

Say: **Behind this sheet is a Lego structure. At the other end of the room there's a matching set of pieces that aren't assembled for each group. You Eyes will stay behind the sheet and whisper to the Ears how to build the structure step by step. The Ears will tell the Feet, who'll walk to the Hands. The Hands will then assemble an identical structure at the other end of the room.**

After the team's Hands have assembled the structures, have the Eyes bring out the original structure and compare it to the newly assembled structures. Ask:

● **How different are the structures? Why?**

● **Who was the most important member of the team?**

● **How important is clear communication among team members? Why?**

Say: **This experience is like being part of the church. All of us have different functions, but all of us are so important that the church is crippled without us.**

Demonstrating Christ's Body—Give kids each a Bible and have them look up 1 Corinthians 12:12-26. Have a different junior higher read aloud each verse. Then give kids each a copy of the "Body Act" handout and assign everyone one of these parts: foot, ear, eye or nose. Read through the script as a group, directing kids to follow the actions in the right column on the handout.

After the skit, ask:
- **What does this passage teach us?**
- **What phrase do you like best?**

Guide the group to say in unison to each person in the group: "___(Name)___, you're a part of this body."

BRIEF BREAK

Serve the snacks kids brought as part of their admission to the lock-in.

SESSION 2: WHAT'S A SPIRITUAL GIFT?

Talent Search—Form teams of three. Give teams each paper, masking tape and a marker. Have teams each list as many talents as they can, each on a separate piece of paper. Then have them tape the papers end to end. The team with the longest list of ideas after five minutes wins.

When time is up, congratulate the team with the longest list. Tape all lists to the wall.

Say: **God gives each Christian a spiritual gift. Spiritual gifts differ from talents, but talents can sometimes be used to express gifts.**

Lists of Gifts—Ask:
- **What's a spiritual gift?**

After kids respond, have them each put their finger on 1 Corinthians 12:27-31 and close their Bible. Give kids each paper and a pencil.

Say: **When all eyes are on me, I'll say "go," and you can open your Bibles to list every gift in that passage. Stand up when you think you've found them all ... Go!**

Let several stand before calling time. Tape a sheet of newsprint to the wall and have kids each say one gift they found in the passage. List these on newsprint.

Say: **There are other lists of spiritual gifts in the Bible. We'll look at two of these. Half of you** (point out which half) **check the**

Body Act

Act out 1 Corinthians 12:12-26, each pretending to be a body part.

Script		Actions
All:	The body is a unit, though it is made up of many members. Though all its parts are many, they form one body. So it is with Christ.	All hug in a huddle.
All:	For we were all baptized by one Spirit into one body.	All hold up index finger.
All:	Now the body is not made up of one part, but of many.	All hold up 10 fingers.
Foot:	If the foot should say, "Because I am not a hand, I don't belong to the body," that would be ridiculous.	Feet gather in a huddle off to the side.
Ear:	And if the ear should say, "Because I am not an eye, I don't belong to the body," that would be downright silly.	Ears gather in a huddle off to the side.
Eye:	If the whole body were an eye . . .	Eyes raise a fist into the air.
Ear:	where would the sense of hearing be? But if the whole body were an ear . . .	Ears cup hands to ears. Ears nod approvingly.
Nose:	where would the sense of smell be?	Noses inhale deeply.
All:	But God has arranged the parts of the body just as he wanted them to be.	All hold hands in a circle and raise hands in the air.
All:	If they were all one part, where would the body be?	All close eyes and bump into each other aimlessly.
All:	As it is, there are many parts, but one body.	All hold hands again.
Eye:	The eye can't say to the hand, "I don't need you."	Hands shake their heads "No!"
Nose:	And the nose can't say to the feet, "I don't need you."	Feet shake their heads "No!"
All:	For God doesn't want the body parts to argue, but rather to care for each other equally.	All point fingers at each other, then hug each other.
All:	That way, if one part suffers, every part suffers with it; if one part is honored, every part rejoices with it.	All hug in a huddle.

list in Romans 12:6-8. The other half check the list in Ephesians 4:11-13. Let's see how many more gifts we can add to our list.

Have kids add to the newsprint list.

When all the gifts from the passages are listed on newsprint, ask:
● **Which gifts are in all three lists?**
● **Why do you think those gifts are listed three times?**

Form pairs. Give pairs each one or more gift descriptions from the "Gift Grading" handout. Also give each pair paper, scissors, tape, a marker, a box and a bow.

Say: **I've given each pair at least one description of a spiritual gift. Demonstrate that spiritual gift with words, illustrations, symbols or drama. For example, create a skit demonstrating your spiritual gift and why we can't live without it. Or draw and write actions that represent this gift and wrap them in the box. Or use the box, bow and paper to dramatize the spiritual gift. Use your imagination.**

Have pairs each present their gift. Warmly applaud each pair.

After the presentations, ask:
● **Why are each of these gifts important?**
● **Why did God give us each different gifts?**
● **How could these gifts be used in the church?**

Matching Talents to Gifts—Have kids look at the lists of talents on the wall and tell how a person could use each talent to express a spiritual gift.

Say: **Ponder which gift or gifts you think God may have given you. We'll discover these during the next session.**

Close with prayer.

STRETCH BREAK

Play Jolly Joints. Have kids each find a partner. Then gather everyone in a circle. Place both stacks of "Jolly Joints Strips" in the center of the circle and have each pair—in turn—draw a strip from each pile. Have partners read their strips, place them back in their respective piles, then connect those two joints between them. For example, if one strip reads "neck" and the other strip reads "ankle," then one partner holds his or her ankle against the other's neck.

Have pairs each continue to draw strips—following new instructions as well as those from previous strips—until it becomes impossible to follow the strips' instructions. The partners with the most joints connected between them win.

Jolly Joints Strips

Photocopy and cut apart both sets of these strips. Mix both sets separately, then set them aside to use during the Jolly Joints game.

knee	neck
jaw	elbow
wrist	finger
shoulder	thumb
hip	toe
ankle	back
knee	neck
jaw	elbow
wrist	finger
shoulder	thumb
hip	toe
ankle	back

SESSION 3: WHAT'S MY GIFT?

Gift Grading—As kids enter, give each a copy of "Gift Grading" and a pencil, and have them each sit as far from anyone else as possible. Say: **Complete this handout about yourself. You'll have an opportunity to talk about what you wrote but no one will see your handout.**

After kids complete the handout, ask:
● **Which gifts got the highest grades?**
● **Which gifts interest you the most?**
● **Which gifts seem best matched to your personality?**
● **Which gift or gifts do you think God has given you?**

Say: **Spiritual gifts aren't offices or ranks, but opportunities to serve, care and grow. Your gifts really don't belong to you. They belong to the people around you. God gave your gifts to you on others' behalf.**

Nothing Without Love—Cue the band members you enlisted ahead of time to play their instruments out of tune. After kids complain and hold their ears, ask:
● **What's wrong with the instruments?**
● **Why did they sound bad?**
● **How is this like us and our spiritual gifts?**
Have kids each read 1 Corinthians 13:1-3.
Ask:
● **What happens when spiritual gifts are expressed without love?**

Invite kids each to share one way they could express a spiritual gift with love. If they aren't sure what gifts they have, suggest they choose ones that seem possible. Point out that even listening to each other share is a way to show love.

The Gifts I See in You—Referring to their "Gift Grading" handouts, guide kids to tell the spiritual gifts they see in each other. Stand behind each junior higher and invite the group to tell gifts or expressions of gifts they see in that person.

Here's My Gift—Lead a time of prayer during which kids offer their spiritual gifts to God. Have kids each pray, completing this phrase: "God, I give you my gift of . . . "

SINGING AND SHARING

Lead kids in singing songs like "We Are One in the Spirit," "We Are One in the Bond of Love," "Blest Be the Tie That Binds," and other

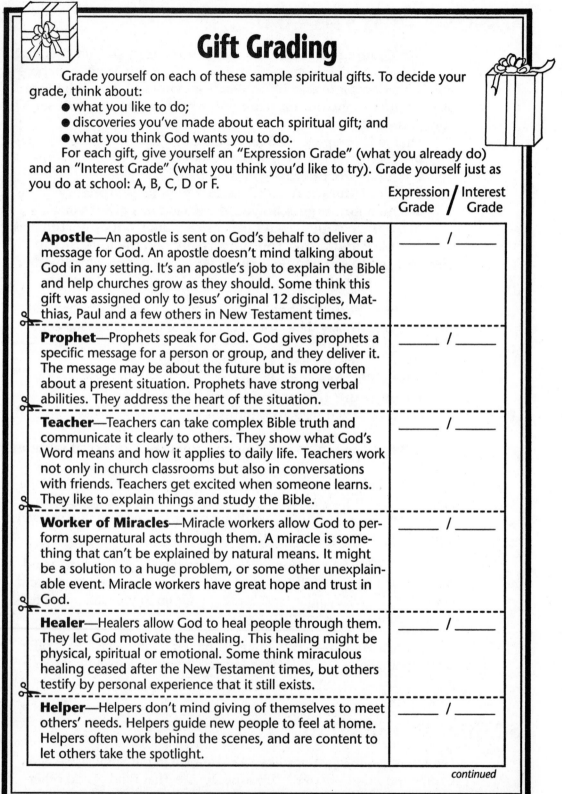

Gift Grading

Grade yourself on each of these sample spiritual gifts. To decide your grade, think about:
- what you like to do;
- discoveries you've made about each spiritual gift; and
- what you think God wants you to do.

For each gift, give yourself an "Expression Grade" (what you already do) and an "Interest Grade" (what you think you'd like to try). Grade yourself just as you do at school: A, B, C, D or F.

	Expression Grade / Interest Grade
Apostle—An apostle is sent on God's behalf to deliver a message for God. An apostle doesn't mind talking about God in any setting. It's an apostle's job to explain the Bible and help churches grow as they should. Some think this gift was assigned only to Jesus' original 12 disciples, Matthias, Paul and a few others in New Testament times.	_____ / _____
Prophet—Prophets speak for God. God gives prophets a specific message for a person or group, and they deliver it. The message may be about the future but is more often about a present situation. Prophets have strong verbal abilities. They address the heart of the situation.	_____ / _____
Teacher—Teachers can take complex Bible truth and communicate it clearly to others. They show what God's Word means and how it applies to daily life. Teachers work not only in church classrooms but also in conversations with friends. Teachers get excited when someone learns. They like to explain things and study the Bible.	_____ / _____
Worker of Miracles—Miracle workers allow God to perform supernatural acts through them. A miracle is something that can't be explained by natural means. It might be a solution to a huge problem, or some other unexplainable event. Miracle workers have great hope and trust in God.	_____ / _____
Healer—Healers allow God to heal people through them. They let God motivate the healing. This healing might be physical, spiritual or emotional. Some think miraculous healing ceased after the New Testament times, but others testify by personal experience that it still exists.	_____ / _____
Helper—Helpers don't mind giving of themselves to meet others' needs. Helpers guide new people to feel at home. Helpers often work behind the scenes, and are content to let others take the spotlight.	_____ / _____

continued

	Expression Grade / Interest Grade
Administrator—Administrators can organize people and things to get a job done. They're good at communicating details and leading others to accomplish a task.	_____ / _____
Tongues—There seem to be two forms of this gift. One is the ability to speak in a foreign language you've never studied so someone who speaks that language can learn about God (Acts 2:3-4). The other is a prayer language that only the Holy Spirit can understand (1 Corinthians 14:2). Some people say this gift ceased after New Testament times.	_____ / _____
Encourager—Encouragers notice and bring out God's best in people. They notice when people are doing right, and praise them for it. They also notice wrong, and gently but firmly correct it. They're sensitive, enthusiastic, inspiring and motivating. Encouragers make people feel good about believing in God and living for him.	_____ / _____
Giver—Givers provide generously for others' needs. Givers seldom feel used but rather gain great satisfaction from giving to others. Givers give money, time, attention and ideas.	_____ / _____
Leader—Leaders guide others to follow God both individually and in groups. Leaders can motivate others and don't mind speaking in front of others. Leaders organize, delegate, mediate and help people understand each other. They help everyone in the group feel needed and important. Leaders elicit trust and fellowship. They tend to have high energy.	_____ / _____
Mercy-Giver—Merciful people are compassionate and sensitive, with hearts that feel others' pain and seek to relieve it. People with mercy see human need and work toward meeting it. They see the good rather than the bad.	_____ / _____
Evangelist—Evangelists motivate non-Christians to become Christians. They're most interested in the beginning faith step—the step of salvation. Evangelists aren't always preachers; they may just be people who talk convincingly about Jesus in everyday life. They make the way to salvation clear and inviting. They lead many to Christian faith.	_____ / _____
Pastor—Pastors are people shepherds. They each take care of a group of believers, walking with their people through good and bad times. Pastors speak words of comfort and of conviction. They seek to guide their flocks on the right path.	_____ / _____

unity songs. Between songs, invite kids to share:
- how it feels to be gifted;
- how I know I'm gifted; and
- what I appreciate about another group member's gift.

ROTATING-PARTNER GAMES

Play rotating-partner card games. Have kids sit in foursomes around card tables and play card games that emphasize cooperation between partners. Time the rounds so all foursomes end at the same time. When time is called, have kids add whatever points they have and declare a winning pair. Award winners each a balloon.

Then have pairs each move to another table and play against a pair they haven't played before. Repeat the game-and-award process. Watch for pairs who seldom win and award "good sport" balloons at the end.

After the games, say: **We don't have to beat someone else or succeed in a certain way to get a spiritual gift. God awards gifts simply because we're Christians.**

ARISE AND EAT!

Assign junior highers each a specific body part—left foot, right foot, right hand, left hand—with which to eat, pack and clean up. For example, only "feet" may hop from place to place, while only "hands" may pick up items such as food or clothing. If a junior higher can't perform a certain function with his or her assigned body part, he or she must ask for help from another person. For example, a left foot would need help from a right hand to eat breakfast.

After breakfast, ask:
- **How did it feel to be limited to one body part?**
- **How do we limit the church when we don't use our spiritual gifts?**
- **How did you feel about helping each other?**
- **How is unity in the body fun? difficult?**

CLOSING WORSHIP

Give kids each a "Gift-Shape Card" to keep in their billfold to remind them to use their spiritual gifts. Provide markers so kids can write their spiritual gifts on their cards.

Gather everyone in a circle and have kids each comment on these subjects:

● a spiritual gift I discovered this weekend;

● what I plan to do this week with my spiritual gift;

● a spiritual gift I notice in someone else; and

● how we can impact our church by living our spiritual gifts.

Read aloud 1 Corinthians 12:27. Close with prayer.

Loneliness and Looks

Loneliness and looks are two of junior highers' main worries. Though junior highers believe in the importance of inner beauty, they live in an "outer" world. Too often kids judge others by how they and their friends look. This focus on appearance contributes to feelings of loneliness and alienation.

To ease both problems, this lock-in challenges kids to deliberately redirect their focus. As they develop their own inner beauty and notice the beauty in others, kids' lonely feelings will ease.

OBJECTIVES

During this lock-in junior highers will:
- watch ugliness characteristics disappear;
- brainstorm causes for loneliness;
- team up with Jesus to ease loneliness;
- choose effective solutions to loneliness; and
- examine how helping others with loneliness eases their own loneliness.

SUPPLY CHECKLIST

You'll need:
- ❑ wrapping paper
- ❑ ribbon
- ❑ toilet paper
- ❑ hairbrushes
- ❑ empty bottles
- ❑ campfire cookout supplies or a pot of boiling water (both optional)
- ❑ "ugly" snacks
- ❑ 3×5 cards
- ❑ scissors
- ❑ assorted decorator icings
- ❑ fast-food sandwich coupons

For every three people you'll need:
- ❑ trash bags
- ❑ newsprint
- ❑ marker
- ❑ masking tape

For each person you'll need:
- ❑ six marshmallows
- ❑ six toothpicks
- ❑ pen
- ❑ Bible
- ❑ blindfold
- ❑ "Jesus' Yoke" handout (page 160)
- ❑ pencil
- ❑ lump of clay
- ❑ "Quick Fix" handout (page 162)
- ❑ envelope
- ❑ "Loneliness Easers" handout (page 163)
- ❑ pocket mirror
- ❑ permanent marker

LOCK-IN PREPARATION

● **Crowdbreaker: Beauty Tips**—In the meeting room, set up a supply table containing these items: wrapping paper, ribbon, toilet paper, hairbrushes, empty bottles and any other props that might work well in a beauty commercial.

● **Optional: Campfire Cookout**—Build a campfire and supply hot dogs, buns, marshmallows, cooking sticks, condiments and drinks.

● **Exercise Break**—Create several sets of alphabet cards by writing each letter of the alphabet on a separate 3×5 card. Make enough cards so each team can have a whole set.

● **I Can Make Myself Less Vulnerable**—Photocopy and cut apart the loneliness easers from the "Loneliness Easers" handout. Place each set in a separate envelope. Tape a copy of the instructions to the outside of each envelope. Create enough sets so each junior higher can have one.

LOCK-IN SCHEDULE

8 p.m.	Crowdbreaker: Beauty Tips
8:30 p.m.	Overview of Rules
9 p.m.	Session 1: I'll Look for Looks That Last
10 p.m.	Ugly Snacks and Lonely Snacks
10:15 p.m.	Session 2: I'll Respond to My Loneliness
11:15 p.m.	Exercise Break
11:30 p.m.	Session 3: I'll Pay Attention to My Vulnerability
12:30 a.m.	Beauty Games
1:30 a.m.	Free Time
3 a.m.	Everybody Sleeps
6:30 a.m.	Breakfast in Bed
6:50 a.m.	Cleanup Race
7:30 a.m.	Closing Worship
8 a.m.	Homeward Bound

THE LOCK-IN

CROWDBREAKER: BEAUTY TIPS

As kids enter, form teams of three. Say: **Develop a commercial for a fool-proof beauty treatment. You may use anything from the supply table or anything else you find in the room.**

After about five minutes, have teams each present their commercial. When all the teams are finished, ask:
   ● **Why do we automatically think beauty's external?**

Kids may blame you for giving "external" materials to work with. Suggest that we come into the world with both internal and external materials to work with but often end up focusing on external. Recall your offer to "use anything in the room," which could've included

compliments, smiles, laughter and more. Ask:
> ● **Why does our society place so much emphasis on looks?**
> ● **How does focusing on looks contribute to loneliness?**

Say: **In this lock-in we'll explore these and other questions.**

SESSION 1: I'LL LOOK FOR LOOKS THAT LAST

Ugliness Review—If you choose to have the Ugliness Review around the campfire, consider roasting hot dogs and marshmallows.

Give kids each six marshmallows, six toothpicks and a pen. Say: **We know inner beauty is what counts, but outer beauty is what we worry about. Create a marshmallow model of yourself that displays all your ugly characteristics. You can highlight ugly toes, ugly elbows or whatever you find ugly about yourself.**

After everyone is finished, have kids each throw their sculpture into a fire or a pot of boiling water.

Ask:
> ● **What happened to the marshmallow when the heat was turned on?**
> ● **How is this like outer beauty?**

Beauty Is a Choice—Have a volunteer read aloud Proverbs 31:30. Ask:
> ● **What fades?**
> ● **What lasts?**

Have kids get back into their teams of three. Give kids each a Bible and have them read Colossians 3:5-17 for qualities of true ugliness and true beauty. Give teams each a sheet of newsprint and a marker. Have them each draw a person that has the passage's beautiful qualities, labeling them on their drawing. Encourage kids to point out not only what the beautiful person has but also what the beautiful person doesn't have.

When drawings are finished, tape them to the wall and have teams explain them.

A Beautiful Person in Action—Read aloud each of these situations. Guide kids to act out how their beautiful people on the wall would respond in each situation:
> ● **Julie's car collided with another and burst into flames. Julie has burns over 50 percent of her body, including her face. She confides to you that she fears no one will ever want to look at her again.**
> ● **Matthew cusses a lot. He says they're the only words that express his strong emotions. You have a gym class with him.**

● **Maria is stunningly attractive and recently became a Christian. You worry that when she comes to youth group she'll attract all the guys' attention.**

● **Reid tells you he doesn't see why he should resist sexual involvement when attractive girls offer it. They use birth control so it's no big deal.**

Close by saying: **When we really understand that outer beauty doesn't last, we can avoid one of the main reasons for loneliness—fear of rejection. Develop the habit of deliberately looking past a person's outer appearance to see the real person inside.**

UGLY SNACKS AND LONELY SNACKS

Serve snacks that look ugly on the outside but taste great on the inside; for example, coconuts or roasted marshmallows.

While kids eat, ask:

● **What might make you hesitate to eat this food?**

● **When do we let people's outer characteristics keep us from enjoying their true beauty?**

SESSION 2: I'LL RESPOND TO MY LONELINESS

Loneliness Debate—Take kids out of the room one at a time. Blindfold them each and tell them they're the only one who'll be blindfolded. Say: **Your task is to learn something new about at least three other people without mentioning anything about your blindfold.**

Then send them into a new room. Blindfold and send all other kids into the new room in the same way. As kids begin to discover that others are blindfolded too, have them remove the blindfolds.

Ask:

● **How did you feel about being blindfolded? about being alone?**

● **What difference did it make to discover that other people were blindfolded too?**

● **You were told not to talk about your blindfold. How is this like loneliness in real life?**

● **Why do we sometimes feel we're the only ones feeling lonely?**

Security Takes Away Loneliness—Ask:

● **What are some causes of loneliness?**

Write kids' responses on a sheet of newsprint. Supplement their responses with these examples: moving to another town, school or church; being rejected; being physically sick; being left out; being physically alone; feeling betrayed by a friend; failing someone.

Give kids each a Bible. Have kids find a solution to each of these causes for loneliness by looking in Psalm 119:22-24 and Matthew 11:28-30. Write kids' solutions next to the problems on the newsprint.

Explain that God is the foundation for security and he guides us to specific solutions to our problems. Invite kids to tell about times they were scorned, felt contempt from others or were slandered. Then read aloud Psalm 119:22-23 a second time.

After the reading, give kids each a copy of the "Jesus' Yoke" handout and a pencil. Have them each write on their yoke how they think Jesus wants them to work through the specific cause of the loneliness they're dealing with.

Stress to kids that Jesus has felt lonely, understands lonely feelings and wants to help kids know what to do. Explain that letting Jesus help with loneliness can keep them from wallowing in self-pity and give solutions that work.

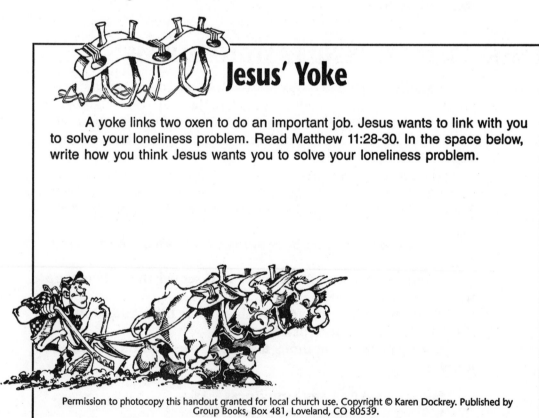

Jesus' Yoke

A yoke links two oxen to do an important job. Jesus wants to link with you to solve your loneliness problem. Read Matthew 11:28-30. In the space below, write how you think Jesus wants you to solve your loneliness problem.

Here's My Loneliness—Give junior highers each a lump of clay. Have them each shape their clay into something that makes them feel lonely. For example, kids might shape clay into a raindrop to show that rain makes them feel lonely.

When kids are finished, have them each share their loneliness sculpture. After each junior higher shares, have the group affirm him or her by saying in unison: **Your loneliness matters to us.**

Take all the loneliness sculptures and press them together to form a ring. Say: **This circle symbolizes our unity. Your loneliness belongs to me and mine belongs to you. We can defeat loneliness through togetherness—whether we're physically together or not.**

Have each junior higher around the circle thank Jesus for giving security and unity to your group.

EXERCISE BREAK

Use your alphabet cards to play one or more of these games:

● Give two or more teams a set of alphabet cards. Call out a word related to looks or loneliness. Award points to the team that can spell it first by each member holding one or more letters up.

● Challenge one team to arrange itself in a word and have the other team tell what that word has to do with loneliness or looks.

● Give kids each one or more alphabet cards. Call out words that deal with loneliness or looks and challenge kids to arrange themselves to form that word.

After the games, say: **Just like single letters put together make up powerful words, when we work together we have the power to take away loneliness and make people feel beautiful.**

SESSION 3: I'LL PAY ATTENTION TO MY VULNERABILITY

I'm Vulnerable When I'm Lonely—Give each junior higher a copy of the "Quick Fix" handout and a pencil. Have kids each complete the handout.

When everyone is finished, have kids each share what they wrote on their "Quick Fix" pill.

Ask:

● **Loneliness makes us vulnerable to certain temptations. What are some of these?**

Say: **For example, someone might use sex or alcohol to block the pain of loneliness. But these "solutions" don't really address the problem. They make us feel better for a while but**

• • • • Quick Fix • • • •

When we get lonely, we want to feel better. This makes us prone to some dangerous "quick fixes." Write in this pill a quick fix that actually causes trouble and why.

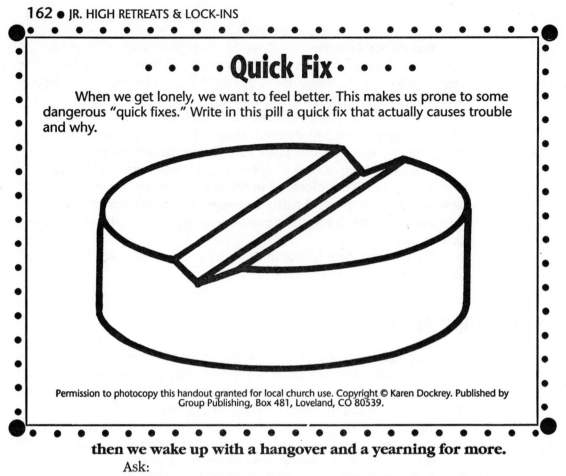

then we wake up with a hangover and a yearning for more.

Ask:

● **What responses to loneliness might lead to real solutions rather than temporary ones?**

I Can Make Myself Less Vulnerable—Have a volunteer read Deuteronomy 30:19-20.

Ask:

● **What loneliness choices might lead to curses and death?**

● **What loneliness choices might lead to life and blessing?**

Give kids each an envelope containing a set of "Loneliness Easers." Have kids each sit on the floor and arrange the loneliness easers in front of them from most- to least-liked.

Ask:

● **Which did you rank #1?**

● **Which did you rank the lowest?**

● **Which loneliness easers can you start using now to help overcome loneliness?**

I Can Use Alone Time—Ask:

● **What's the difference between being alone and being lonely?**

Loneliness Easers

Place these loneliness easers in order of their effectiveness for you. Remember to make choices that lead to life and blessing (Deuteronomy 30:19-20).

Talk to a friend.

Read the Bible.

Stay by myself for a little while.

Read a good book or magazine.

Listen to a happy song.

Invite a friend to go do something.

Figure out why I'm lonely.

Talk to someone about how I feel.

Write my feelings in a poem, story, diary or letter.

Concentrate on someone else's problems.

Play my guitar or other instrument.

Find something to do to keep busy.

Other: _____.

After kids respond, form teams of three and give each team tape, a pencil and a stack of 3×5 cards. Say: **Think of interesting activities to do during alone time. Write one on each card and tape the cards end to end. Make your idea chain longer than any other team's chain.**

After a few minutes, have teams each hold up their idea chain and read their ideas to the group. Applaud the longest. Tape the chains to the wall as reminders of great ideas to do when alone.

I Can Make You Less Vulnerable—Say: **Another way to deal effectively with loneliness is to reach out to other people.**

Ask:

● **How can you reach out to others?**

After kids respond, gather everyone in a circle of chairs. Say: **Let's see how many conversation-starters we can think of. As we go around the circle, each of you say a conversation-starter such as "Hi! How are you?" If you can't think of one within 15 seconds, then you must stand on your chair until we come around to you again. No one may repeat what someone else has said. We'll continue until we run out of conversation-starters.**

Start the game and continue until everyone is standing on a chair.

After the game, have everyone sit down. Ask:

● **How can choosing to stay lonely get in the way of your happiness?**

● **How can choosing to stay lonely get in the way of others' happiness?**

Say: **Loneliness isn't a sin, but choosing to stay that way can be. It can become a form of self-centeredness. Address your loneliness each time it pops up and then choose to reach out and help others with their loneliness.**

BEAUTY GAMES

To help kids work off extra energy, have them play one or more of these silly beauty games:

Beauty Contest—Form teams of four to six. Give teams each assorted decorator icings and challenge them to make up one of their team members—either male or female. Hold a beauty contest for the most attractive, most colorful and most creative makeup jobs.

After the game, ask:

● **How is beauty like a game?**

● **Why do we find it so hard to resist the game?**

● **How might the world be better if we had no mirrors?**

Beauty Charades—Play Charades with inner-beauty qualities that kids submit. Suggest they draw from Galatians 5:22-23 and Romans 12:9-21.

After the Charades, ask:

● **Why is it harder to notice these qualities both in ourselves and others?**

● **What happens to these qualities when you face tough times?**

BREAKFAST IN BED

Serve simple breakfasts such as breakfast sandwiches and juice in the sleeping rooms to allow kids time to relax before getting packed.

CLEANUP RACE

Have kids form pairs or trios. Challenge groups to clean up and pack up as a team. Offer free sandwich coupons from a local fast-food restaurant to the team who fills a trash bag the fullest or cleans its area the best.

CLOSING WORSHIP

Give each junior higher a pocket mirror as a token of the lock-in. Give kids each a permanent marker and have them write this sentence around the border: "You are beautiful because God made you" (Psalm 139:14).

Say: **Every time you look in this mirror, remember to focus on your inner beauty and realize you're never alone.**

Guide kids to thank God for creating them and never leaving them alone.

Peer Pressure

Junior highers usually respond to talk about peer pressure in one of two ways:

- they claim peer pressure doesn't exist; or
- they blame their poor conduct on it.

Few take peer pressure seriously enough to harness it for good. This lock-in is designed to equip junior highers to recognize and harness the power of peer pressure.

OBJECTIVES

During this lock-in junior highers will:

- discover it's okay to want people to like them;
- determine ways peers influence them for good and bad;
- pinpoint actions that can harness peer pressure for good; and
- brainstorm ways they can use positive peer pressure.

SUPPLY CHECKLIST

You'll need:
- ❏ posterboard
- ❏ scissors
- ❏ pipe cleaners
- ❏ masking tape
- ❏ newsprint
- ❏ "Pressure Bag" handout (page 171)
- ❏ paper bag
- ❏ 3×5 cards
- ❏ pizza ingredients
- ❏ breakfast supplies

For each person you'll need:
- ❏ Bible
- ❏ balloon
- ❏ permanent marker
- ❏ pizza ingredients
- ❏ "See the Good in Each Other" handout (page 175)
- ❏ pencil
- ❏ paper

LOCK-IN PREPARATION

● **Create a Friend**—Before the lock-in, set up "creation" tables along one wall of the meeting room. On the tables, display these supplies and any others you think are appropriate: posterboard, scissors, pipe cleaners, masking tape and markers.

Tape a copy of the "Perfect Friend Instructions" on page 169 to the wall above each table.

● **Pressure Opposites**—Photocopy and cut apart the "Pressure Bag" handout. Make enough copies so each junior higher can have at least one strip. Place the strips in a paper bag.

● **Remember the Rewards**—Write these words from Proverbs 3:3-6 on separate 3×5 cards. Make a set for every four kids: Love, Faithfulness, Bind, Write, Win, Favor, Trust, Lean and Straight.

LOCK-IN SCHEDULE

8 p.m.	Crowdbreaker: Create a Friend
8:30 p.m.	Introductions
8:45 p.m.	Session 1: When We Help Each Other
9:55 p.m.	Stretch Break
10 p.m.	Session 2: When We Hurt Each Other
11:15 p.m.	Build Your Own Pizza
11:45 p.m.	Eat Pizza!
12:15 a.m.	Session 3: Together We Can Do It!
1:30 a.m.	Free Time
3 a.m.	Everybody Sleeps
7 a.m.	Rise and Shine
7:15 a.m.	Breakfast
7:30 a.m.	Closing Worship
8 a.m.	Go Home!

THE LOCK-IN

CROWDBREAKER: CREATE A FRIEND

As kids arrive, send them to the creation tables. Have them each read the instructions taped to the wall above their table and begin working on creating the perfect friend.

After all the kids have arrived and are working on their creations, tape a sheet of newsprint to the wall. After a few more minutes, have kids each present their friendship creation. On the newsprint, list the characteristics kids mention as they do their presentations.

INTRODUCTIONS

Say: **We all crave good friends and loving acceptance. This yearning for closeness is the way God made us.**

Ask:

● **What happens when we fulfill this yearning with good friendships?**

● **What happens when we don't find the friends we've just described?**

Say: **During this lock-in we'll discover ways to give and receive happy and healthy kinds of love.**

SESSION 1: WHEN WE HELP EACH OTHER

Find the Positive—Ask:

● **What's your first reaction when you hear the term "peer pressure"?**

● **Why do people make such a big deal of it?**

Have a volunteer read aloud Hebrews 10:24-25.

Ask:

● **Is peer pressure always bad? Why or why not?**

Write Hebrews 10:24-25 on a sheet of newsprint. Have volunteers come up and underline all the action words in the passage.

Ask:

● **How would you use these actions to encourage others to follow God? to find happiness?**

Perfect Friend Instructions

Use the items on your table to create a model of the perfect friend. The model can have moving parts or be one solid piece. It can look like a person or just be a conglomeration of symbols. Be prepared to explain what makes your model "perfect."

Pressure Opposites—Hold up the Pressure Bag and say: **Sometimes it's hard to tell positive from negative pressures. Let's practice identifying them. In this bag are some of both. As we pass the bag around, each of you take a pressure strip from the bag. Read your pressure, then tell us whether it's positive or negative, and what its opposite is. For example, the opposite of the positive pressure of inviting someone to sit with you would be to ignore that person or make fun of him or her.**

Let the person with the birthday closest to today go first.

After everyone has responded, ask:

● **What are some other positive or negative pressures?**

● **What are the opposites to these pressures?**

Say: **Think of positive responses whenever negative pressures occur. For example, when a friend asks if he or she can cheat from your paper, say "No, but I'll study with you next time."**

Invite kids to share more examples. Then close with prayer, asking God to help kids make wise decisions when faced with positive or negative pressures.

SESSION 2: WHEN WE HURT EACH OTHER

Move to the Left—Seat kids in a circle. Say: **I'm going to make a series of statements. If the statement I read is true for you, move one seat to the left. If someone's already sitting there, just sit on his or her lap.**

Read aloud these statements:

● **You're wearing blue jeans.**

● **You remembered to bring your Bible.**

● **You have brown eyes.**

● **You have green eyes.**

● **At least once in your life, you did something good just because someone else was doing it.**

● **You've done something negative to get attention.**

● **You've pressured a friend in a positive way.**

● **You've blamed peer pressure for something that was really your decision.**

● **You're ready to talk about a new form of pressure rather than creating pressure by sitting on each other.**

If kids don't move, play a few more rounds by making up new statements for kids to respond to.

Remember the Rewards—Say: **The Bible offers many responses that can help us resist negative pressure. It also re-**

Pressure Bag

Photocopy and cut apart these strips, and place them in a paper bag. Create enough so each junior higher can have one.

✂ -

Invite someone to sit with you.

✂ -

Make fun of someone who sits alone.

✂ -

There's a great party tonight with plenty of beer. Let's go!

✂ -

Let's have an alcohol-free party.

✂ -

Invite someone to church.

✂ -

Ignore people who don't go to your church.

✂ -

Study together.

✂ -

Cheat from someone's paper.

✂ -

Cut someone down.

✂ -

Compliment someone.

✂ -

Decide not to have sex.

✂ -

Pressure your date to have sex.

✂ -

Start an anti-drug campaign in your school.

✂ -

Sell drugs to your friends.

✂ -

minds us of rewards for doing right. To discover some of these responses and rewards, we'll play Pass-a-Word. Keep your Bible open for help.

Form groups of five—two pairs and one moderator. Seat groups with partners facing each other and the moderator to the side. Follow these steps:

1. Have the moderator show one person in each pair a card you made from the list on page 167. The person in the first pair gives a one-word clue to his or her partner to help the partner guess the word.

2. The partner guesses by looking at Proverbs 3:3-6 and choosing one of the words. If the guess is correct, the pair gets 10 points. If not, the clue-giver in the second pair gives another one-word clue for nine points. Continue to alternate giving clues until someone guesses the word or until the point value is zero.

3. The moderator keeps score and is the final judge of whether a guess is correct.

After the game, read aloud Proverbs 3:3-6.

Ask:

● **What's your favorite response? Why?**
● **What's your favorite reward? Why?**

Pressure Pop—Give kids each a balloon and a permanent marker. Have them each write on their balloon a negative pressure situation they've faced recently. As kids finish, have them tape their balloons to a wall.

When everyone is finished, have kids each explain their balloon. Then have kids each pick a balloon other than their own and name a way to deflate the pressure written on that balloon. After someone names a way to deflate the pressure, have him or her pop that balloon.

After all the balloons are popped, ask:

● **Which peer-pressure popping strategies do you find easiest to use?**
● **What keeps the pressures from popping back up?**
● **How can we help each other pop pressures?**

Say: **The best prevention for negative peer pressure is positive friends.**

Invite kids to comment. Have a volunteer read aloud Hebrews 10:24-25 as a closing meditation.

BUILD YOUR OWN PIZZA

Set up pizza crusts with sauce along tables. Provide toppings for kids to create their own pizzas. Topping possibilities include: cheeses, sausage, hamburger, pepperoni, green pepper, onions, ham, olives and any other ingredients you want to try. Encourage kids to use the ingredients to create faces, designs, symbols and more. While the pizzas cook, allow kids free time in the meeting room.

SESSION 3: TOGETHER WE CAN DO IT!

Personal Portrait—Lay out a sheet of newsprint. Give kids each a marker and have them sign their name on the newsprint in the shape of something that describes their personality. For example, someone might write their name in the shape of a flower to show they're happy or fun-loving.

After everyone has signed the newsprint, say: **Each of your signatures is unique. In the same way, the way you provide love, friendship and support is unique.** Ask:

● **How do you think you influence people?**

Say: **Return to your signatures and draw ways you influence others. For example, if you influence others by helping them go the right way, then you might draw a compass or a pointer.**

After kids finish, have them each explain their drawing. Affirm each person's efforts.

I Thank God for You—Give junior highers each a copy of the "See the Good in Each Other" handout and a pencil. Have them each find a partner and complete the handout.

Here are the answers: 1-c; 2-a; 3-b; 4-b; 5-d; 6-c; 7-a; 8-b; 9-a; 10-c. After reviewing the answers, ask:

● **Which type of encouragement do you need most? Why?**
● **Which type do you give most easily? Why?**

Here's What We Want—Give kids each paper. Have them each rewrite Philippians 1:3-11 as they think Paul would write it to them today. Form pairs and have kids each read aloud their paraphrase to their partner.

Quick Draw—Have kids form two lines facing each other. Then have them sit on the floor. Say: **Pair up with the person sitting across from you. Each of you name a good goal you want to achieve. Then have your partner try to name a way he or she**

can create pressure to help you reach your goal. For example, if your goal is to make an A in math, your partner could offer to study with you.

Repeat the process two or three times, allowing kids each to name two or three goals. If your group is small, have pairs go one at a time. If not, have pairs go simultaneously, then get together and share.

Close with prayer.

BREAKFAST

Serve a breakfast made from pressure: waffles and orange juice. Say: **Pressure made the batter turn into great waffles. Pressure also squeezed oranges into juice. In the same way, pressure can bring out the good in you.**

CLOSING WORSHIP

Read aloud James 1:22-25. Say: **Living God's way brings the freedom and happiness we want. Let's help each other on this journey toward happiness.**

Give kids each the name they drew on the newsprint in Session 3. Guide kids in offering sentence prayers that they'll each become a positive-pressure friend and say no to negative pressure.

See the Good in Each Other

In each category, match the beginning of the action with its ending. Read Philippians 1:3-11 to get started.

Past

We can notice and compliment what good things friends have already done for God.

1. I thank ...

2. I always pray ...

3. Your partnership ...

a. with joy.

b. in the gospel from the first day.

c. my God every time I remember you.

Present

We can encourage friends to do good things for God.

4. He who began a good work in you ...

5. I have you ...

6. All of you share ...

7. I long for all of you ...

a. with the affection of Christ Jesus.

b. will carry it on to completion.

c. in God's grace with me.

d. in my heart.

Future

We can motivate friends to strengthen their obedience and faith in God.

8. And this is my prayer: that your love ...

9. So that you may be able to discern ...

10. And may be pure ...

a. what is best.

b. may abound more and more in knowledge and depth of insight.

c. and blameless until the day of Christ.

My Place to Belong

Kids need to belong. They'll do almost anything to achieve it, possibly including hiding their beliefs and compromising their values. This lock-in, built around Ephesians 4:16, seeks to equip junior highers to understand and express their need to belong in healthy ways. Only as junior highers accept each other and reach out with Jesus' kind of love will they discover what it means to belong.

OBJECTIVES

During this lock-in junior highers will:
- see their value as a part of the group;
- get to know others in the group;
- memorize Ephesians 4:16;
- recognize they have the power to help others belong; and
- act out ways belonging can solve specific problems.

SUPPLY CHECKLIST

You'll need:
- ❏ masking tape
- ❏ newsprint
- ❏ sandwich supplies
- ❏ soft drinks

For every four people you'll need:
- ❏ 10 building blocks
- ❏ "Love Builders" situation (page 185)

For each person you'll need:
- ❏ "Glad You're Here!" information sheet (page 178)
- ❏ pencil
- ❏ "Belonging Quiz" (page 180)
- ❏ paper cup
- ❏ marker
- ❏ Bible
- ❏ three candies
- ❏ paper
- ❏ 3×5 card
- ❏ "Memorization Strips" (page 183)

LOCK-IN PREPARATION

● **Belonging Building**—Set up a table full of building blocks. Provide enough so every four kids can have 10 blocks.

● **Ephesians Demonstration**—Photocopy and cut apart the "Memorization Strips" so each junior higher can have one strip.

● **Making Belonging a Reality**—Photocopy and cut apart the "Love Builders" situations so every four kids can have one situation.

● **Create a Taco**—Before the lock-in, assign kids each a separate item to bring for making tacos, nachos and drinks.

THE LOCK-IN

WELCOME AND RETREAT INTRODUCTION

As junior highers enter, give each a copy of the "Glad You're Here" information sheet and a pencil. Have them each complete the sheet and return it to you.

LOCK-IN SCHEDULE

8 p.m.	Welcome and Retreat Introduction
8:30 p.m.	Session 1: Part of the Group
9:30 p.m.	Break
9:45 p.m.	Session 2: My Part in Belonging
10:45 p.m.	Belonging Snack
11 p.m.	Building Belonging
12:01 a.m.	Midnight Madness
2 a.m.	Create a Taco
3 a.m.	Bedtime
7 a.m.	Rise and Shine
7:15 a.m.	Breakfast and Affirmation
8 a.m.	Home

GLAD YOU'RE HERE!

Complete this handout and return it to your leader.

My name:

I like to be called:

My address:

My phone number:

My birthday:

My school and grade:

I love to:

But I hate to:

After kids finish the sheet, give them each a copy of the "Belonging Quiz" and have them each complete it. When everyone is finished, review the answers: 1. a,b,c; 2. a,b,c; 3. c,d; 4. c,d; 5. a,b; 6. c,d.

SESSION 1: PART OF THE GROUP

The Shape of Isolation—Give kids each a paper cup and say: **Shape this cup to show how someone feels when he or she is left out or isolated.**

When kids finish, have them each explain their cup. Then have them all throw their cups to the middle of the floor.

Ask:

● **What do you see?**

After kids respond, say: **I see a jumbled mass of unrelated objects. Our group may feel like this sometimes, but it doesn't have to be this way. We can make our group a place where each cares about the other.**

Invite kids to share what they'd like to see happen in the area of unity in the group.

Assembling a Group—Tape a sheet of newsprint to the wall. Give kids each a marker and a Bible. Say: **Write the words of Ephesians 4:16 in large letters on the newsprint and decorate the newsprint.**

When the poster is complete, count the number of people present and tear the poster into that many pieces. Shuffle the pieces and instruct kids each to take a piece and write their name on the back. Together, assemble the puzzle with the verse side up.

Ask:

● **How have you demonstrated this verse by putting it back together?**

● **What if one of you was missing?**

● **What if someone else entered after the puzzle was torn?**

Turn the puzzle name side up.

Ask:

● **How does this side of the puzzle make the puzzle more important?**

● **What do we do to make others feel unwanted?**

● **How can we make people feel they're necessary?**

Lay the puzzle pieces aside for use later in the Closing Worship.

Can't Give It Away Fast Enough—Give each person three candies. State these two rules:

Belonging Quiz

Circle all the correct responses.

1. During this lock-in, we'll . . .
   a. experience belonging.
   b. help each other feel we belong.
   c. listen to each other.
   d. perform the Vulcan mind-meld.

2. We'll also . . .
   a. study hard.
   b. play hard.
   c. eat a lot of food.
   d. dismantle the church.

3. And we'll . . .
   a. play our tape players.
   b. launch each other out of vintage civil war cannons.
   c. participate in all sessions.
   d. share openly.

4. We must stay together as a group until the event is over because . . .
   a. we're anticipating a medical quarantine.
   b. we've already been quarantined.
   c. the church is responsible for our safety so it needs to keep tabs on us.
   d. it's more fun to stay around our friends.

5. At midnight we'll go bowling. We'll be expected to . . .
   a. have fun.
   b. enjoy others.
   c. bowl with our toes.
   d. get 10 strikes each.

6. The adults are here to . . .
   a. spoil our fun.
   b. spoil our food.
   c. answer questions.
   d. love us.

1. If someone offers you candy, you must take it but you may not eat it.

2. You must give away all your candy, one piece at a time.

Enjoy the fun and jot down what your kids say. Call time after a few minutes.

Ask:

● **How easy was it to give away your candy?**

● **How easy was it to accept candy?**

● **What feelings did you have? When were you pleased? frustrated? happy? sad?**

● **Did any of you want to hide? participate less? participate more? Why?**

● **How does this activity demonstrate belonging or the lack of it?**

Supplement kids' comments by repeating some of the things they said during the candy giveaway. Say: **If all of us concentrate on giving love, each of us will feel overwhelmed with care and we'll realize we belong.**

SESSION 2: MY PART IN BELONGING

Picture Me—Line junior highers up according to birthdays. Have the first four form one group, the second four another, and so on. Give kids each paper and a marker. Say: **Draw a picture that represents you. It can include stick figures, symbols, words or elaborate drawings. Include your feelings, worries, hopes, interests—whatever matters to you.**

After several minutes, have kids each share their drawing in their group. Then have kids each tell each person in their group something in his or her drawing they like.

After kids share, have kids form new groups of four. Have groups each repeat the sharing process. Continue to rotate groups until everyone has shared with everyone else.

It Depends on the Situation—Ask:

● **How does sharing with everyone make you feel you belong?**

● **What situations make you feel you don't belong?**

Have a volunteer read aloud Luke 6:27-36.

Ask:

● **Reaching out to new people is risky. Why is it worth the risk?**

Have kids share a time someone reached out to them.

Ask:

● **How did they reach out to you?**
● **How did you feel about it?**

Ways You've Done It Unto Me—Say: **Tell one way you'd like to live Luke 6:31. For example, listen, say hello, show interest or ask someone new to sit with you.**

After kids share, say: **Now tell ways you've seen each other live Luke 6:31. How have you seen someone in this group treat others as he or she wants to be treated?**

Be sure each junior higher is mentioned at least once.

I'm Part of the Solution—Give kids each a 3×5 card and a pencil. Have kids each write their name vertically and name a way— beginning with each letter of their name—they'll build unity in this group. For example:

Know more about people's needs.
Yak more with people I don't know well.
Learn to make friends.
Eat with new kids more often.

After kids are finished, have them each share what they wrote. Read aloud Ephesians 4:16. Emphasize that during this session kids have demonstrated a group that "builds itself up in love." Encourage them to make it a habit!

BELONGING SNACK

As junior highers come through the snack line, give some of them bread, some of them lunch meat, some of them cheese, some of them knives, some of them mayonnaise or mustard, some of them chips, some of them ice, some of them soft drinks, some of them cups and some of them plates. Don't give any instructions; just observe the way they handle the predicament, and jot down what they say and do.

After the snack, ask:

● **Why do you think we distributed sandwiches this way?**
● **How did you work together?**
● **What frustrations did you experience?**
● **How did your attitude change because of what someone did or didn't do?**
● **How did you demonstrate the body of Christ? betray it?**

SESSION 3: BUILDING BELONGING

Belonging Building—Form teams of four. Say to the teams: **Go to the supply table, pick up 10 blocks, take them to the location**

of your choice and build a tower. The only rule is that you may not bend your elbows or knees.

When teams finish their assignment, ask:
- **What did you think about this challenge?**
- **Why are joints important?**

Read aloud Ephesians 4:16 again.

Ask:
- **What would a "ligament" in Christ's body be?**
- **What does it mean for our group?**
- **Which parts of our group work best?**
- **Which need work?**
- **How could we improve?**

Ephesians Demonstration—Give kids each at least one strip from the "Memorization Strips." It's okay if more than one person has the same strip.

Say: **These strips are parts of Ephesians 4:16. Stand in correct order, then memorize your portion on your strip.**

When junior highers are in correct order, have them each say their part of the verse. Then have them repeat the verse again, this time having certain kids remain silent. Remark how everyone is

Memorization Strips

Photocopy and cut apart these strips so that each junior higher has at least one.

From him

the whole body,

joined and held together

by every supporting ligament,

grows and builds itself up in love,

as each part does its work.

Ephesians 4:16

needed for the group to memorize the verse.

After reviewing the verse a few more times, call for volunteers to recite the verse by themselves.

When most kids have the verse memorized, ask:

● **What made memorizing this verse easy?**

● **Could we have memorized the verse if certain people refused to participate? Explain.**

● **How does this experience relate to unity in our group?**

Direct junior highers to tape their verse portions in order to the wall.

I Matter—Have kids each find a partner, turn back to back and link elbows. Have partners sit on the floor and then stand while linked.

As pairs succeed, have them each join with another pair—this time all four people linking arms—and repeat the activity. Continue to merge teams until the whole group is linked. Having the whole group stand with arms linked may take several tries, but keep trying until it works. Ask:

● **When was it easier to perform the linked sitting and standing?**

● **Why does it get harder when more people are added?**

● **How is this like belonging?**

Say: **Just as everyone had to work together to make this exercise work, we must also work together to reach out to more people so our group will grow close and loving. Unity isn't always easy, but by supporting each other, we can all feel like we belong.**

Making Belonging a Reality—Form teams of four. Give teams each a situation from the "Love Builders" situations. Have teams each dramatize their situation in two ways:

● a way that could tear down; and

● a way that builds up in love.

Have teams present their dramas. Praise each team.

Say in closing: **I pray you'll recognize God's power as he loves through you. Concentrating on accepting others helps us forget our fears of being accepted.**

MIDNIGHT MADNESS

Travel to a late-night bowling lane or skating rink. If these are impractical or unavailable in your area, lead a game tournament at the lock-in site.

Love Builders

Photocopy and cut apart these situations so each team of four has one.

- ✂ -

Situation #1: An obnoxious person starts coming to your junior high fellowships. This person does stupid stuff to get attention and is driving everyone crazy. You know there are problems at home.

- ✂ -

Situation #2: A member of the group who doesn't come very often is injured in an auto accident. He or she will be out of school for a month.

- ✂ -

Situation #3: One member of your group seems to get quieter and quieter. Finally he or she stops coming. You don't want to be nosy but you fear there's something wrong.

- ✂ -

Situation #4: Pat calls one group member all the time to talk and suggest things to do. The group member wants to be nice but is getting tired of Pat.

- ✂ -

Situation #5: A person with a questionable reputation starts coming to your junior high group. Your parents tell you not to spend time with him or her because you might be influenced. This person seems genuinely interested in spiritual matters.

- ✂ -

Situation #6: One person in the group feels that no one else likes him or her. It's not true, but he or she is driving people away by harping on it. How can you help this person feel like part of the group?

- ✂ -

Situation #7: Other junior highers in your group make fun of a certain person because he or she is poor. If you stand up for this person you fear they'll reject or ridicule you.

- ✂ -

CREATE A TACO

Display a table with the fixings for tacos, nachos and drinks kids brought with them to the lock-in. Explain how each person was necessary to make the food good. Thank each junior higher for contributing to the success of the taco snack.

CLOSING WORSHIP

Gather kids in a circle. Invite kids to recite all or part of Ephesians 4:16. Have them share how they've seen this verse in action during the lock-in.

Give kids each their puzzle piece from Session 1 and a hug. Guide the group to say to each person as you give the piece: "We're glad you're in our group, (name of person)."

Guide kids to pray together by completing these statements:
- "Lord, belonging means so much to me because ..."
- "Lord, knowing you want me to belong in your church ..."
- "Lord, help me to show others that they belong by ..."

Life After Death

Death is the furthest thing from junior highers' minds—or is it? Surveys show that one of junior highers' main concerns is the death of a parent. Many junior highers also fear nuclear war will wipe out the world before they grow up. When someone their own age dies from an illness or an accident or when a relative dies, junior highers wonder how they'll die and what'll happen to them after death.

This lock-in raises these and other questions junior highers ask about death. Then it guides kids to find biblical answers to their questions.

OBJECTIVES

During this lock-in junior highers will:
- recognize that fears of death are normal;
- discover specific truths about God that can ease their fears;
- examine images of heaven from Revelation; and
- apply faith to their fears.

SUPPLY CHECKLIST

You'll need:
- ❑ 3×5 cards
- ❑ masking tape
- ❑ songs about death or heaven
- ❑ stereo
- ❑ pizza
- ❑ brick
- ❑ shoe box
- ❑ bop bag
- ❑ roll of aluminum foil
- ❑ cassette recorder
- ❑ blank cassette tape
- ❑ volleyball net
- ❑ beach ball
- ❑ sundae ingredients
- ❑ sweet rolls

For every two people you'll need:
- ❑ "Life After Death Letters" (page 189)
- ❑ "Find the Mistakes" handout (page 193)

For each person you'll need:
- ❑ "Sharesheet" (page 191)
- ❑ pencil
- ❑ paper
- ❑ marker
- ❑ Bible
- ❑ four identical "Image and Truth Trade" cards (page 195)
- ❑ ring

LOCK-IN PREPARATION

● **Fear Easers**—Write these references on separate 3×5 cards: Psalm 23:4; John 14:1-4; 1 Corinthians 15:20-22; 1 Thessalonians 4:14; Hebrews 9:28; and Hebrews 11:1. Then tape each under a different chair in the meeting room. Make enough copies so every chair has a verse taped to it.

● **Music Evaluation**—Before the event, survey kids to find popular Christian or secular songs that deal with death or heaven. Get recordings of three or four of these songs.

● **I Have a Foundation**—Get a bop bag from a local toy store. A bop bag is an inflatable, free-standing punching bag that's weighted on the bottom so it won't topple. Inflate the bop bag and set it aside until the activity.

● **Bible Images of Heaven**—Photocopy and cut apart the "Image and Truth Trade" cards so each junior higher will have four identical cards.

● **Sit-Down Volleyball**—Hang a volleyball net indoors so the top of the net is about four feet off the floor.

LOCK-IN SCHEDULE

8 p.m.	Crowdbreaker: Life-After-Death Letters
8:30 p.m.	Lock-In Introduction
8:45 p.m.	Session 1: Fears
10 p.m.	Snack Break: Warm It Up
10:30 p.m.	Session 2: Foundation
11:30 p.m.	Break
12 a.m.	Session 3: Faith
1 a.m.	Sit-Down Volleyball
2 a.m.	Ice Cream Sundaes
3 a.m.	Everybody Sleeps
6:30 a.m.	Rise and Shine Race
7:30 a.m.	Closing Worship
8 a.m.	Head for Home

THE LOCK-IN

CROWDBREAKER: LIFE-AFTER-DEATH LETTERS

As kids arrive, have them form pairs to play Life-After-Death Letters. Give pairs each a copy of the game and a pencil. Say: **Circle as many words as you can and jot down each word you circle. Words can be vertical, horizontal, diagonal, backward or forward.**

After a few minutes, have pairs each count their words. Have everyone give the winning pair a round of applause.

Ask:

● **Without looking, who can repeat the four truths printed on your handout?**

LOCK-IN INTRODUCTION

Ask:

● **How old do you think you'll be when you die?**

Life After Death Letters

Circle all the words you can find in this block of letters. Words can be vertical, horizontal, diagonal, backward or forward. You can count plural words twice—once in singular, once in plural—and words within words. For example, the word "Jesus" also contains the word "us."

```
T D T P K M A L A D Y Q H O F N I W D B A
F E A R O F D E A T H I S N O R M A L S T
J E S U S E A S E S F E A R O F D E A T H
C H R I S T I A N S L I V E F O R E V E R
E T E R N A L L I F E B E G I N S N O W U
U V D R D C B L O T O L S N A E B Y O S E
E G T A P R E T E P S R L U O Z O B T T N
Z O G N I N E T R O H S E L B A T E G E V
```

● **What do you suppose you'll die of?**

Say: **Though we may not want to think about it, we'll all die someday unless Christ returns first. Statistics indicate that 10 out of every 10 people die. This lock-in addresses this universal experience and the fear that surrounds it.**

SESSION 1: FEARS

My Fears and Your Fears—Form groups of four. Give kids each a copy of the "Sharesheet" and a pencil. Have kids each complete the sheet and share their answers with their group.

When groups are finished, call everyone together and ask:

● **What did you find similar about your fears? different?**
● **What else would you like to share about the fear of death?**

Fear Easers—Give kids each a Bible. Have kids each look under their chair for a Bible promise you taped there earlier. Say: **Look up your verse and tell how it eases one of the fears on your "Sharesheet."**

Music Evaluation—Play excerpts from some of your kids' favorite songs that address death, fear of dying or heaven. Use Christian and secular songs.

After you play each excerpt, ask:

● **What does the song say about dying? about heaven?**
● **What does it say to do about our fears?**
● **Does this song agree with the Bible? If so, how?**
● **How does it disagree with the Bible?**
● **If you were rewriting the song, what would you say?**

Favorite Foundational Truths—Review the four foundational truths you studied earlier:

1. Fear of death is normal;
2. Jesus eases fear of death;
3. Christians live forever; and
4. Eternal life begins now.

Have kids each choose their favorite truth and tell why they like it. Ask:

● **If you believed these truths, how would your life change?**

SNACK BREAK: WARM IT UP

Serve hot and cold pizza.

Ask:

Sharesheet

Complete each sentence by circling your favorite response or writing your own. Share your answers with your group and explain why you responded as you did.

1. I fear death most when . . .
   a. someone I know dies.
   b. I think about it.
   c. I have an accident or near accident.
   d. _____.

2. What I fear most about death is . . .
   a. missing out on something here on Earth.
   b. the process of death itself.
   c. not getting to say goodbye to people I love.
   d. _____.

3. I think I'll die . . .
   a. in my sleep.
   b. a painful death.
   c. a slow death.
   d. _____.

4. I feel most comfortable talking about death . . .
   a. with a friend.
   b. with my parent.
   c. with another Christian.
   d. _____.

5. I wish I could know . . .
   a. how I'll die.
   b. when I'll die.
   c. exactly what heaven is like.
   d. _____.

6. Being a Christian reduces my fear of death because . . .
   a. I can talk to Jesus about it.
   b. I know I'll go to heaven.
   c. I know I'll see my loved ones again in heaven.
   d. _____.

● **Which pizza do you prefer?**
● **Why does warmth make a difference?**

Say: **Life with Jesus is like this warm pizza. He makes life the way it's supposed to be. The cold pizza has the same ingredients as the hot pizza, but has no "life." Likewise, life with Jesus brings true life before and after death.**

SESSION 2: FOUNDATION

My Epitaph—Give kids each paper and a marker. Have them each tear a tombstone shape and write on it what they'd like to see as their own epitaph. Say: **An epitaph is what people say about you on your tombstone.**

When kids are finished, have them each read their epitaph. Have kids each write their name on their tombstone and give it to you. Say: **During this session, think about what actions and attitudes would lead people to say this about you.**

Jesus Is My Foundation—Say: **Let's study the reason we know we'll have eternal life.**

Have kids form pairs and give each pair a copy of the "Find the Mistakes" handout. Give kids each a Bible. Say: **One of you correct the mistakes while the other reads the Bible passage.**

When pairs have finished, read aloud the "Find the Mistakes" handout, challenging kids to yell "Stop!" when you read a mistake. As kids correct mistakes, add your comments. Ask:

● **How do we know we have eternal life?**
● **What mistakes do people make about death?**

Set out a brick and a shoe box. Choose a volunteer to stand on the brick. After he or she has successfully stood on the brick, ask:

● **What held you up—the brick or your faith? Explain.**

Choose a second volunteer to stand on the shoe box.

When the shoe box collapses, ask:

● **Why didn't the shoe box hold you up? Was your faith in the box too weak?**
● **How much faith would you need to make the shoe box support you?**

Say: **Faith is only as good as the object in which it's placed. No matter how much faith I have in the shoe box, it'll still collapse. But because Jesus rose from death, we know God will raise Christians from death too.**

Guide kids to read 1 Corinthians 15:54-58.

Ask again:

● **How do we know we have eternal life?**

Find the Mistakes

Circle and correct each mistake by comparing this with 1 Corinthians 15:12-22.

But if it was preached that Christ has been raised from the dead, how can some of you say that there was resurrection of the dead? If there is no resurrection of the dead, then only Christ has been raised. And if Christ has been raised, our preaching concentrates on the present and so does your faith. More than that, we are then found to be false witnesses about God, for we have testified about God that he raised Christ from the cross. But he did not raise him if in fact Christians are not raised. For if the dead are not raised, then Christians are not raised either. And if Christ has not been raised, your faith is more important; you are no longer in your sins. Then those who have fallen down in Christ are asleep. If only for this life we have hope in Christ, we are to be honored more than all men.

But Christ has possibly been raised from the dead, the firstfruits of those who have fallen asleep. For since life came through creation, the end of life comes also through a man. For as in Abraham we all die, so in Christ all will die again.

I Have a Foundation—Set out the bop bag you brought with you. Give junior highers each a chance to knock it over.

Ask:

● **What forces threaten to knock us over?**

● **How do we know we won't be wiped out?**

Say: **We can push the bop bag down but it won't stay down. Similarly, injury, disease and even death can't keep us down forever. We're eternal beings.**

Making My Epitaph Come True—Redistribute the tombstones kids made, and say: **Write on the back of the tombstone actions and attitudes that'll make your epitaph come true.**

Have volunteers each share what they wrote on their tombstone. Close with prayer.

SESSION 3: FAITH

My Image of Heaven—Pass around a roll of aluminum foil. Have kids each tear off a piece and shape it into their image of heaven. This could be something they plan to see there, something they plan to do there or simply a symbol to represent heaven.

When kids have finished, have them each explain their sculpture.

Ask:

● **What will be in heaven?**

● **What won't be in heaven?**

● **Where do we get our images of heaven?**

● **Do you ever fear heaven might be boring? Why or why not?**

After several respond, say: **Heaven is beyond any words we could use to describe it. It's a place of happiness and God's presence. He'll make sure we don't get bored!**

Bible Images of Heaven—Have kids each turn to Revelation 21. Say: **This chapter is full of images and truths about heaven. To learn some of these, lets play a trading game.**

Shuffle the deck of "Image and Truth Trade" cards you made before the meeting. Deal each junior higher four cards. Say: **You now have four cards. Trade cards one at a time, without showing the card you're trading, until everyone has four cards that match.**

After everyone has four matching cards, have kids each look up the verse in Revelation 21 that tells about the image on their cards. Have kids each read aloud the verse and tell how that image or truth describes heaven.

Image and Truth Trade

Photocopy and cut apart these cards so that each junior higher will have four identical cards.

New Heaven (Revelation 21:1)	New Earth (Revelation 21:1)
Holy City (Revelation 21:2)	New Jerusalem (Revelation 21:2)
God is with men (Revelation 21:3)	Wipe every tear from their eyes (Revelation 21:4)
No more death or mourning or crying or pain (Revelation 21:4)	Everything is new (Revelation 21:5)
Spring of the water of life (Revelation 21:6)	I'll be his God and he'll be my son (Revelation 21:7)
A great, high mountain (Revelation 21:10)	Brilliance like a precious jewel (Revelation 21:11)
A high wall with 12 gates (Revelation 21:12)	Foundations decorated with every kind of precious stone (Revelation 21:19)
God's glory gives it light (Revelation 21:23)	No more night there (Revelation 21:25)
Nothing impure will ever enter it (Revelation 21:27)	Those who enter have names written in the book of life (Revelation 21:27)

Presence of God—Set out a cassette recorder with a blank cassette tape. Say: **We're going to make a tape sharing our assurances of eternal life. Then whenever we're feeling down or worried or afraid, we can listen to this tape and be encouraged. I'll make enough copies so each of you can have one to keep.**

Pass the recorder around and have kids each share a fact about eternal life and how life after death helps them feel secure. Suggest starter sentences such as:

- I know there's eternal life because ...
- Because Jesus has promised me eternal life ...
- Eternal life makes earthly life better by ...

When everyone is finished, rewind the tape and play it for the kids.

Faith Eases Fear—Give kids each a 3×5 card and a pencil. Have them each write on the card a fear they have. When kids finish, collect the cards, shuffle them and redistribute them to new owners. Say: **Look at your card and tell how Jesus and his promise of eternal life can help you overcome that fear.**

After kids respond, close with prayer.

SIT-DOWN VOLLEYBALL

Play Sit-Down Volleyball by having teams sit on the floor and play regular volleyball with a lowered net and a beach ball. Team members must remain seated while the ball is in play.

ICE CREAM SUNDAES

Provide sundae ingredients and let kids assemble their own.

Give kids an hour or so to make and eat sundaes, and to talk with friends.

RISE AND SHINE RACE

Rouse slumbering kids and challenge the guys to beat the girls to breakfast and vice versa. To win, all male or female group members must be completely dressed, luggage and sleeping bags packed and at the door, and sleeping rooms cleaned up. Award sweet rolls to the winners. Serve the losers buttered toast. Let kids share if they're willing.

CLOSING WORSHIP

As kids enter the worship area, give each a ring. It can be any kind of ring, even a curtain ring.

Affirm kids' responses as you ask each person:

● **How is a ring like eternal life?**

Read aloud Revelation 21:4 and 1 Corinthians 15:54-55. Have kids each offer a sentence prayer about God's salvation and eternal life. Close by naming each junior higher, asking God to reveal his salvation to him or her.

Have kids keep their rings as reminders of God's gift of eternal life.

PRACTICAL PROGRAMMING
RESOURCES FROM

GROWING A JR. HIGH MINISTRY
By David Shaheen

Ministering to junior highers requires unique approaches and well-trained leaders. You'll find a wealth of practical ideas and suggestions for strengthening your ministry. Discover ...

- Ministry-building leadership tips
- How junior highers think
- Ways to get parents involved
- How to build positive relationships

Plus, scores of programming ideas for meetings, special events, discussion-starters, attendance-builders and more. Get proven help for your junior high ministry.

ISBN 0-931529-15-8 $12.95

INSTANT PROGRAMS FOR YOUTH GROUPS 1, 2, 3, 4
From the editors of Group Publishing

Get loads of quick-and-easy program ideas you can prepare in a flash.

Each meeting idea gives you everything you need for a dynamic program. Step-by-step instructions. Material lists of easy-to-find items. Dynamic discussion-starters. And ready-to-copy handouts to involve kids.

Each book gives you 17 (or more) meeting ideas on topics that matter to teenagers ...

1—Self-Image, Pressures, Living as a Christian
2—Me and God, Responsibility, Emotions
3—Friends, Parents, Dating and Sex
4—Tough Topics, Faith Issues, Me and School

With all four books, you can keep a year's worth of program ideas at your fingertips—ready to tap instantly.

Instant Programs for Youth Groups 1, ISBN 0-931529-32-8 $7.95
Instant Programs for Youth Groups 2, ISBN 0-931529-42-5 $7.95
Instant Programs for Youth Groups 3, ISBN 0-931529-43-3 $7.95
Instant Programs for Youth Groups 4, ISBN 1-55945-010-X $7.95

10-MINUTE DEVOTIONS FOR YOUTH GROUPS
By J.B. Collingsworth

Get this big collection of ready-to-use devotion ideas that'll help teenagers apply God's Word to their lives. Each 10-minute, faith-building devotion addresses an important concern such as:

- Love
- Failure
- Faith, and more
- Peer pressure
- Rejection

You'll get 52 quick devotions each complete with scripture reference, attention-grabbing learning experience, discussion questions and a closing. Bring teenagers closer to God with these refreshing devotions—perfect for youth activities of any kind!

ISBN 0-931529-85-9 $6.95

FUN OLD TESTAMENT BIBLE STUDIES
By Mike Gillespie

Offer your teenagers an understanding of the Old Testament with 32 eye-opening Bible studies. Each session helps teenagers experience the drama of the Old Testament—then apply what they've learned to their own problems and concerns.

Your kids will love the active-learning experiences when you teach ...

- Persistence—by building a precarious tower of cards
- Justice—by making sculptures that represent consequences of wrong actions
- Creation—by telling the story of Creation through pantomime

Plus, you'll get step-by-step help to prepare and make the Old Testament unforgettable to your young people.

ISBN 0-931529-64-6 $12.95

CREATIVE RESOURCES FOR YOUR YOUTH MINISTRY

YOUTH MINISTRY DRAMA & COMEDY
By Chuck Bolte and Paul McCusker

Here's a fun, hands-on approach to using drama and comedy in your youth ministry. You'll get step-by-step help for putting on plays—and 20 super scripts you can use now.

Plus, you'll pick up time-saving tips on how to ...
- Run smooth rehearsals
- Use promotion ideas that work
- Improve directing skills
- Write your own scripts
- And communicate effectively with your actors

Use drama and comedy for meetings, worship services, retreats, special events and more. Turn your group into a drama troupe with Youth Ministry Drama & Comedy.

ISBN 0-931529-21-2 $12.95

QUICK SKITS & DISCUSSION STARTERS
By Chuck Bolte and Paul McCusker

Here's a new tool for grabbing attention and building faith in youth groups. Help your teenagers build confidence and self-esteem. Improve communication skills. Practice teamwork. And examine issues from a Christian perspective. You'll get complete instructions, 26 simple warm-up exercises, 18 quick skits and thought-provoking discussion questions with matching biblical references.

ISBN 0-931529-68-9 $9.95